simply
green

simply
green

Easy, Money-Saving Tips
for Eco-Friendly Families

**Melissa Seligman
and David Seligman**

CITADEL PRESS
Kensington Publishing Corp.
www.kensingtonbooks.com

CITADEL PRESS BOOKS are published by

Kensington Publishing Corp.
850 Third Avenue
New York, NY 10022

All Kensington title, imprints, and distributed lines are available at special quantity discounts for bulk purchases for sales promotions, premiums, fund-raising, educational, or institutional use. Special book excerpts or customized printings can also be created to fit specific needs. For details, write or phone the office of the Kensington special sales manager: Kensington Publishing Corp., 850 Third Avenue, New York, NY 10022, attn: Special Sales Department; phone 1-800-221-2647.

Printed on recycled paper.

First printing: March 2009
10 9 8 7 6 5 4 3 2 1

Printed in the United States of America

Library of Congress Control Number: 2008936775

ISBN-13: 978-0-8065-3112-0
ISBN-10: 0-8065-3112-6

This book is dedicated to

My parents. For teaching me the beauty of simplicity
and for instilling the need to always feel the lush, green grass
beneath my bare feet.

—Melissa

and

To our children, Amelia and Elijah.
May you both grow to be green giants
and learn to leave little footprints on this Earth.

—David

CONTENTS

Contents

YOUR LIVING ROOM: LIVE IT

YOUR BEDROOM: GREEN DREAMS

YOUR BATHROOM: LATHER, RINSE, REUSE

Part Three: Nurture the Green Genes   133

*Fun, crafty, and educational ways to plant green seeds of change
in our children.*

Part Four: Work It   163
*Simple ways to maintain your input and
recycle your output at work.*

Part Five: Take It to the Streets   179
*Simple ways to sit back, relax,
and smell the clean air while on vacation.*

ACKNOWLEDGMENTS

We would first like to thank our friends and family for always supporting us. Thank you for allowing us to hibernate while we wrote and collaborated. We love all of you, and without your patience and willingness to tolerate our green ventures, this book would not exist.

A very special thank you goes to our agent, Kate Epstein, for bringing this book to us. Thank you, Kate, for always having an open ear and a willing spirit. This book wouldn't reflect our lifestyle or personality without the sharp editing and delightful wit of our editor, Danielle Chiotti. Thanks to you, Danielle, for seeing the fun in going green and for helping to sculpt this book into something our children will be very proud of.

Thank you, Amy Pyle, for stepping in and answering any crazy questions without hesitation or reservation. We would also like to thank Jill Boltin for creating such a sleek, innovative cover design.

This book wouldn't be complete without thanking our source of inspiration. Thank you, Amelia and Elijah, for giving us a reason to care about our Earth and the problems facing the next generation. We hope you always see the fun, beauty, and constant marvels that our Earth has to offer. Keep it simple and green, but more than anything, keep it fun!

"Opie, you haven't finished your milk. We can't put it back in the cow, you know."

—Aunt Bee Taylor, *The Andy Griffith Show*

Green Can Be Simple

When David and I first met, he had a long goatee, rode a bike as his only source of transportation, avoided corporate businesses as much as possible, and wore oversized, hand-me-down clothes from his roommate. He was working on a degree in environmentalism, and I was working on creating a career after college. We spent weeks at a time camped out in the hills of Kentucky, and we both professed a love of nature. His love, however, went far deeper than mine.

He rarely bathed so as not to waste water, and I loved long luxurious baths filled with bubbles and bath salts. He walked around his apartment in the winter wrapped in a blanket and a ski hat to avoid using extra heat, while I preferred wearing shorts in my overly toasty apartment. He spent hours trying to help me see the error of my ways, and I wasted my breath trying to get him to relax his rigid viewpoints.

Fast forward to nearly ten years later. We now have two young children, David is in the U.S. Army, and I am a stay-at-home mother/writer. Although I still take baths every once in a while, short showers have mostly replaced them. And David has realized that our children can't walk around all winter in their snowsuits to avoid turning up the heat. With our desire to compromise, make ends meet with two ever-growing children, pay off two college loans and a truck loan, survive on one steady income, and still do our share to protect the Earth, we learned how to apply very simple and extremely effective principles in order to achieve a productive, and, most importantly, a sustainable green lifestyle.

The first lesson we had to learn is that we can't do everything and we can't feel guilty for not trying. Sure, dropping modern society to live on an eco-friendly commune would be fun and adventurous, but we decided that we wanted to teach our kids that it isn't necessary to remove yourself from society in order to create change within it. We do not need to draw that line in the sand between modern society and environmentalism. It doesn't have to be one way or the other. You can merge the two with simple, efficient, green changes. That means that our very happy children often wear secondhand clothes, play with secondhand toys, and sleep in nearly new beds. They know the value of giving to charity, and they enjoy planting and working in and eating from their own garden.

With Hollywood and the popular media leading the green movement, there is this overwhelming feeling that if you aren't buying hybrids, eco-friendly clothing, and front-loading washers, and installing solar panels in your home, then you are not concerned about our environmental crisis. That couldn't be farther from the truth.

Why buy a new washer when yours isn't broken? Why throw away our perfectly good clothing in order to replace it with more expensive organically woven clothing? We have no desire to throw away or trash what isn't broken in our house. And we don't expect you to, either.

We do not wish to berate you. We don't want to preach to you. What we do want to do is meet you where you are and be your friends and your neighbors, standing beside you and encouraging you on your own discovery of a green lifestyle that is right for you.

You don't have to have money and, most importantly, you don't have to spend money in order to make very simple and very real changes that affect the environment on a daily basis. Simple things like turning off your lights, maintaining your vehicle, and using your imagination and your "trash" in greener ways will lead to positive change.

Our vision of changing this world doesn't involve inducing fear and Armageddonesque images with depressing statistics. It involves uplifting encouragement and the desire to pull the rich and poor together to stand side by side in this fight to save the world that we all share. The tools for living greener already exist within your home and your lifestyle, and we'll show you how to keep your current lifestyle while giving it a green makeover. Most of all, we want to encourage you to make the simple decision to care.

Through our simple and inexpensive tips for living more environmentally friendly, you will see that going green isn't about how much money you have. It isn't about prestige. It isn't about how green you are compared to your neighbors. It is about working together, making simple and important changes toward a better life. For all of us. You don't have to do everything to be green. You just have to do *something*.

This book is really the springboard into your green journey, so if after reading these tips, you find yourself wanting more "somethings" to do, check out the additional reading resources at the back of the book.

PART ONE
Take It Outside

Q*uick and creative tips for your backyard environment.*
Before we jump into great ways to reuse rainwater or your broken dining room chairs, stop and take a moment to give yourself a pat on the back. You are taking a very important first step in going green: You are reading this book. And when the first pull of living a green lifestyle begins to tug at your mind or to creep into your conversations, it is important to step back and take a moment to decide if going green is right for you. Although it isn't necessary to do everything suggested in this book in order to live a productive, green lifestyle, it is necessary to find your "green motivational fuel."

Green motivational fuel is not the answer to gas prices, but rather your reason for going green. What is it that initially sparked your interest? Do you want to stop paying so much for gas? Do you feel a need to clean up the environment for the sake of your children or your grandchildren? Do you want a cleaner park for your beloved pet? Or, do you just want to roll back those numbers on your energy bill?

You may find that green motivational fuel outside, waiting to be tapped into. Sure, sleeping on the ground and roughing it through the mountains may not sound like your personal octane level of green motivational fuel. And it doesn't have to be. Taking the time to just step outside for a meal, play in your backyard with your children, or teach them new and inventive ways to conserve our resources may create your own unique outdoor version of green motivational fuel. Whatever it is that causes you to step outside, smell the fresh air, and look for ways to green your environment, take that motivation and put it toward simple, affordable, and efficient ways to make a difference in your own backyard. Don't worry, you won't have to hug any trees. Well, not unless they introduce themselves first.

1. Branch Out

Taking a moment to gather your thoughts and untangle your mind is one of the easiest and greenest ways to save energy. With cell phones constantly ringing, computers announcing incoming e-mails, televisions shouting at you from room to room about new detergents, underwear, and low-interest loans, who couldn't use a moment to step away and gain perspective? Our society is more demanding, more technologically entwined, and more exhausting than ever before. Who hasn't sat through dinner at a restaurant while listening to the next table's cell phone conversation or the continuous clickity-clack of laptop keys?

Take a moment and shut it all down. Stop answering the call of the phone and turn off the computer. Go back to the basics. Step outside and take a deep breath. You may think that there is nothing to do outside, but the truth is, there is nothing you can't do outside. Here are a few ways to get started:

- Carry your plates from the kitchen to your backyard and have a picnic. You will relax, unwind, and breathe deeper than you ever thought possible.
- Take your children to the park. Break that television habit and

get them addicted to fresh air. Blow bubbles with them. Dig in the dirt with them. They will only want you around for a little while, so take the time to tune them in and to tune out your buzzing and beeping world.

- Sit on your back porch and thumb through a magazine. Sip on lemonade.
- Arrange snuggle sessions under the stars. Nothing spells romance like a little star gazing.
- Rake leaves, pile them, and let your kids jump to their hearts' content.

These may seem like simple and obvious things to do. They are meant to be. But slowing down is often much harder said than done. Turning off your television, computer, radio, or telephone will truly free you from your spinning, chaotic electric world and will open your eyes to the world outside.

Take a book outside with you. Take the newspaper. Take a hot cup of coffee on a cold winter's day. Take nothing. Take a nap. Take anything and everything. Take whatever will relax you and doesn't require an outlet.

If you only have one free moment during the day, choose to take that moment outside. Make the time to breathe, feed your brain with radiant oxygen, and relax. If you make the choice to turn off the computer, the kitchen lights, the television, or the radio, you will not only conserve energy, but also find a moment to observe and partake in the world we are all trying to save.

Great Green Tip

Have you ever watched a thunderstorm in action or stopped to smell the roses, only to find yourself wondering why these miraculous moments aren't celebrated? Well, actually they are!

And you can celebrate them, too. April 22 is Earth Day. Take the time to stop, check into the world around you, and thank Mother Nature for all she provides. Most likely, others will be stopping and celebrating as well, so take the time to band together, smell the roses, and enjoy the miracles of nature.

2. Squash the Litterbug

Imagine for a moment that you are outside, walking through a beautiful park. The sun warms your shoulders, and only a few clouds dance in the sky. Birds chirp in the distance, and the soft grass whispers beneath your feet. Lush green trees dance in the wind, and an intoxicating aroma engulfs you as gorgeous wildflowers bask in the sunlight. Now, imagine looking just to your right, next to the colorful wildflowers and lush emerald green. There, nestled in the billowing grass you find . . . trash?

One of the most disturbing issues of our society is our willingness to drop our trash without a second thought. According to the social activist group Green-CT:

- Cigarette butts, coming in at a staggering number of 4.5 trillion, are the most littered items around the world. Within those little butts there is a form of plastic that will exist in the environment for 10–12 years.
- Plastic six-pack rings are responsible for the deaths of 6 million sea birds a year and over 100,000 marine mammals. They also take 450 years to decompose.
- Plastic bags take 10–20 years to decompose.
- According to the Natural Resources Defense Council, our oceans are littered with plastic food bags, foam cups, aluminum cans,

glass, and cigarette butts, just to name some items. Who wants to swim in that?

If those numbers aren't bothersome enough, according to the science and physics website, PhysOrg.com, our tendency to litter, especially where plastics are concerned, has created a floating trash island twice the size of Texas in the Pacific Ocean between San Francisco and Hawaii. According to the same website and to Chris Parry with the California Coastal Commission in San Francisco, the "Great Pacific Garbage Patch" has been around since the 1950s and is comprised of 80 percent plastic. It weighs more than 3.5 million tons.

What makes this not just the marine animals' problem, but ours as well, is that according to the nonprofit environmental organization Algalita Marine Research Foundation (AMRF), the tiny pieces of plastic floating in the water wind up in filter-feeding marine life, like jellies and salps, as well as fifty species of fish and many turtles. That may not seem like a human issue, but before you take that scrumptious bite of fish, imagine how the plastic is making its way up the food chain and possibly into your belly. That thought alone makes litter not just an environmentalist's problem, but a people problem.

Although these numbers are alarming and sad, there are few ways to police our country's habit of littering. However, there are ways to fight it.

- *Squash the litterbug.* If you see someone littering, and you have the gumption, then, by all means, say something. Some people actually seem embarrassed and polite when they are confronted, while others may not care. Even if you choose to say something, don't always expect immediate results. While you may not be able to create change right away, you're providing others with the opportunity to think about their actions.

- *Stoop and scoop.* If confrontation isn't your thing, the simple and less abrasive approach is to merely pick it up when you see it. Although it may seem frustrating to have to pick up someone else's trash, you are, after all, making the choice to do something about it. It is unfair, but the most important thing to remember is that you are leading by example. Before you leave your house, take a litter bag with you (preferably a bag you are choosing to reuse rather than throw away) and use it to pick up litter.
- *Take action.* Every state or local community has different ways to handle littering. Contact your community, local, or state government office to find out if and how you can report litterbugs. You can also visit the website of the nonprofit organization, Keep America Beautiful: www.kab.org/site. This website will help you find an organization near you that will help remove the litter from your area.

The next time you take a walk in your favorite park or a swim in your nearest waterway, take a look around and do your part to clean it. Not only will you be choosing a greener lifestyle, but you will also be making a statement. You may not be able to squash every litterbug, but you can do your share to help exterminate them.

3. Plant a Garden

Okay. So we don't all have green thumbs. But, if you have a willing spirit, and even a small patch of grass, you can save money and energy by growing a little bit of your own food. Even if houseplants seem to wilt under your care, with a little help from nature, it is possible to grow a variety of fruits and vegetables in your own backyard.

If planting a garden conjures images of continuous rows of corn and cucumbers with men and women milling about doing back-breaking work and taking time only to remove their large straw hats to wipe sweat from their tired brows, do not fear.

Take that overgrown image and shrink it to a small square of soil. Start with one item. If you can eat your weight in tomatoes, then try growing them. If you love zucchini, there's no better place to grow it than your own backyard.

Think you can only eat tomatoes when they're red and ripe? Think again! If you find yourself overrun with tomatoes, consider this recipe your tasty reward:

Fried Green Tomatoes
2 fresh, firm, green tomatoes from your garden
1 cup flour
1 cup cornmeal
Basil (or sage, or pepper, or your favorite seasoning)
One egg and ¼ cup milk
Vegetable oil

1. Wash and cut the tomatoes into ¼ inch slices.
2. In a medium bowl, combine flour and cornmeal to create a half-and-half mixture. Add basil or your favorite seasoning.
3. In a separate bowl, mix the milk and the egg together.
4. Pour vegetable oil into an iron skillet and let it heat.
5. Dip the tomato slices into the egg and milk mixture and then coat them in the flour and cornmeal mixture.
6. Drop the coated slices into the oil and cook until brown.
7. Cool and serve with cocktail sauce or a horseradish and may-onnaise mixture.

Planting and eating from your own garden can be a rewarding experience, even if you have only the palest of green thumbs. You will be surprised with the amount of pride you feel when you take that first bite of a ripened, personal fruit of your labor.

Great Green Tip

Put your energy in your feet. We all know that walking is good for our bodies, but it is also one of the greenest ways to run errands. If you live a stone's throw from your local shopping center or supermarket, leave your car at home and enjoy your environment. The next time you need to hop in the car to drive a mile, make the decision to hoof it instead.

4. Get an Old Set of Wheels

Let's all take a step back here for a moment and think about our very first bicycle ride. Clear your head, close your eyes, and remember that feeling of accomplishment. Feel the wind in your hair. Hear the sound of the tires as they move over the pavement. Feel the ache in your thighs and the sensation of flying as you take your hands from the handlebars, spread your arms out into the wind and throw your head back while the wind blows past your smiling face.

For most of us, riding a bicycle was one of the most exhilarating and fundamental building blocks of our childhood. And for most of us, those wheels have long been put away. We have replaced those two wheels for the more expensive four-wheeled, six-wheeled, and eighteen-wheeled vehicles. But according to the Union of Concerned Scientists website, those extra wheels are responsible for the majority of the air pollution in the United States, causing more than half of the carbon monoxide, a quarter of the hydrocarbons, and a third of the nitrogen oxides in our atmosphere. With all those wheels moving and creating more smog and smoky air, why not try reducing the number of wheels out there?

Take a simple and green tip from your own childhood and break out your old bike from its hiding place in your garage. If you don't have a bike, borrow one. Everybody knows someone who bought a bike in hope of using it. If they are using it, then search your local yard sales. You don't have to go buy a brand new bike. At least not until you are sure that you will use one again.

Start out simple. Ride your bike to a neighbor's house or to the local market for a few groceries. Most places readily provide bike racks for your convenience. Ride your bike with your family. Ride around your neighborhood until you can find that child inside you that still longs for the wind on your smiling face. Once you wake that part of yourself up again, you are ready to make a simple change in your life.

Use your bike for errands. Ride it to work if you can. The more you ride, the less you drive and the less you contribute to the pollution problem. The more you ride, the less gas you use. The more you ride, the healthier you become.

Take a simple and green tip from your former self. Step back into your own past and back onto your bike. That wonderful feeling of flying never goes away.

5. Green Grass Pass

Summer just wouldn't be summer without the sound of lawn mowers buzzing in the distance. Manicured lawns are a hallmark of modern suburban living. However, with 54 million American homes using a gas-powered mower every week, the U.S. Environmental Protection Agency (EPA) states that lawn mowers and garden equipment are responsible for 5 percent of our current air-pollution issues.

One of the most obvious ways to reduce this number is to use a manual reel mower. Manual mowers are practical and efficient, not to mention nostalgic, and they provide the immediate satisfaction of a well-mowed lawn, and sore arms, legs, and shoulders to boot! But, although it is a great way to get exercise and is completely safe for the environment, how many of us are willing to stare down one or two acres of billowing grass with a small manual piece of steel mower in our hands? Not too many. Especially when the majority of us have been spoiled by gas-powered mowers. One of the ways to attack this dilemma is to create a sharing program with your friendly neighbors. Pool your money together and invest in a manual mower. Then, take turns mowing each other's lawns. Yes, it is a workout, and you are doubling your mowing time, but consider the fact that next weekend, you can sit back and relax while your neighbor takes the steel wheel.

If this idea doesn't appeal to you, or if you already have a fully functioning gas-powered mower, you don't have to stop using it. Instead, take a moment to decide if your lawn mowing is necessary. If a portion of those 54 million homes decided to skip one week of mowing, wouldn't it seem possible to decrease air pollution? Weekly mowing isn't necessary. It isn't really practical. Think about the weekend you take off as a stolen opportunity to spend more time with your family and friends, or to have a few moments of precious alone time.

For those of us who enjoy a freshly cut lawn, there are just as many that feel the need to trim hedges and use a weed-eater for all wayward and pesky intruders. Invasive weeds surrounding the fence or garden always seem to plant themselves just beyond the reach of the chopping blades of the mower. So, for many of us, weed-eating and trimming are closely related to mowing. The greenest way to attack this issue is to use brute force. If possible, pull the weeds by hand. It can be extremely gratifying to literally see that weed's journey ended by the grip of your hands. And when it comes to trimming the hedges, use manual clippers. Sure, it takes longer and it requires more work, but it also provides instant satisfaction in seeing and feeling your accomplishment.

If that just isn't an option for you, or if you just really need the sound of a mower and a uniform, freshly cut look, then consider some of the EPA's cleaner options and recommendations:

- Ask around about the new, cleaner gasoline equipment on the market.
- Consider the propane and solar options that are available.
- Use electric equipment, which is better than gas-powered machines. Electrically powered lawn and garden tools produce little or no pollution from exhaust emissions or through fuel evaporation.
- Decrease your lawn area by planting a garden, more trees, or shrubs.

Giving yourself a week away from lawn mowing is a simple way to do your part to conserve energy and reduce emissions that result in air pollution. Take the time you would normally spend on your lawn and spoil yourself. You may experience guilt when you see your neighbor's newly cut grass, but after a few times of blissful indulgence, you may find yourself enjoying an ice-cold beverage and kicking up your heels while your neighbor labors away in the hot summer sun. Eat, drink, and be merry, for tomorrow the grass will still be there. Go ahead, be bad and pass on your weekly cut.

6. Green Means Stop

After all that hard pushing and pulling the mower through your lawn, it would seem that your work is complete. However, after mowing, do you find yourself fighting the urge to pull the hose out to water the grass? One of the telltale signs of summer is sprinklers working overtime to water the lawns of the neighborhood. We all like fresh, green, soft grass. It is appealing and pleasing to the eye. Definitely more so than the lawns filled with brown grass, showing the signs and damage of a summer of drought, and waiting for that quenching burst of rain to reawaken the flowers and scorched earth. There is no doubt watered lawns are pretty. But what price are we paying to keep them lush and green?

Let's let go of global warming issues for a moment. Let's not discuss environmentalism or recycling or reusing. Let's take a moment and just reflect on people. One of our basic needs as humans is water. There is no avoiding it. Our bodies require it and can't function without it. So, does it make sense to sit in an air-conditioned house, comfortably watching television, while a sprinkler spreads one of our most basic needs all over a lawn in order to change the color from brown to green? Especially when there are people in this world dying from the lack of water. According to the EPA's "Water-Efficient Landscaping" article on their website, of the 26 billion gallons of water used daily in the United States, outdoor water use is responsible for 7.8 billion gallons, or 30 percent.

Of course, the ground and our plants and gardens do need quenching. But, if we aren't living on a farm, working hard to produce food from the earth, what need is there really in having vibrant, green front lawns? Yes, green is prettier. Green is pleasing. However, going green and working to make a difference in this world doesn't always mean having a green lawn.

You don't have to completely give up on having a green lawn. But, if you do feel a pull to help stop water shortages, start saving on your water bill, and start ensuring one of your basic needs as a human, you may want to consider a few changes when maintaining your lawn:

1. You can always let the Earth take care of itself. Mother Nature has a way of maintaining her own needs. It is only when we feel the need to "help" that she is overworked and off task. So, if you aren't a farmer whose income is dependent upon keeping your land fertile, put the hose down and step away from the sprinkler.

2. If you have rain gutters, try collecting buckets of overflow and storing the water in a sealed container. When it comes time to water, pull out your own natural reserve and give the lawn a drink where applicable.

3. If collected rainwater isn't an option for you, or if your lawn is too big to water by hand, you can always manually spray your lawn with your hose. According to the EPA, which quotes the American Water Works Association Research Foundation's outdoor end use study, households that sprayed manually used 33 percent less water than the average household.

4. Use timed sprinklers that do not run continuously.

5. For you early birds, get the worm and get to watering before the sun becomes intense. If you water when the sun is in full effect, a lot of your effort will evaporate.

You can still go green and have green grass. However, going green does require giving up the habit of kicking back with a glass of cold lemonade while the sprinkler does all the work.

Great Green Tip

Looking for a fun, inexpensive, green gift idea for that special friend? Try giving the gift of gardening. Buy a window box planter, soil, seeds, a watering can, and a pair of gardening gloves. Put all but one seed package in the planter. Wrap the planter with newspaper (which can later be used for mulch, weeding, composting, or wrapping paper for another gift) and use twine to tie it all together. Punch a hole in the seed pouch, and use it as a gift tag for your lovely, green gift. Not only will you be giving a gift that is thoughtful and unique, but also one that will continue to grow and blossom, along with your friendship.

7. Weed Out the Pests

If you have a garden, or you are new to the gardening world, weeds and pests are among the most troublesome issues of raising food, flowers, or plants. The dilemma: To kill, or not to kill? If you break it down even further: To spray or not to spray?

One of the first knee-jerk reactions when seeing bugs, slugs, or any sort of creepy crawlers is usually to kill them. Better them than you, right? Well, not exactly. Although there are some pesky bugs, flies, and worms that can be a nuisance to your pretty greenery, there are also just as many helpful little critters out there that you may not want to kill. Many bugs, snakes, frogs, lizards, worms, bees, or spiders in your garden have specific jobs, and their presence suggests that Mother Nature is actually working with you rather than against you. However, weeding out the friendly critters from the flower killers can be a bit tricky.

Among the friendly critters are our lovely spider friends and lady-bugs. Ladybugs are the heroes of the garden because they love to eat aphids, which, although not detrimental to a plant, do remove sap and often leave your leafy friends in great distress if you choose to take no preventative action. Although ladybugs are often cute enough to leave alone, spiders are also good and healthy for the environment. They are out for blood, but thankfully they prefer insects rather than human flesh. But a harmless garden spider is, in fact, your friend. A spiderweb in your garden means that spiders are hard at work, catching insects that could otherwise damage your plants and flowers.

If you do find yourself in a situation where hornworms have attacked your tomato plants, or slugs or ants are destroying your garden bed, there are countless natural and organic options for your gardening needs:

- Allow nature to take its course. Sure, you may have little patience while you watch tiny bugs crawling and gnawing on your leaves, but if you sit back and wait, you will see those friendly winged creatures flying in to save the day.
- Plant horsemint. It has a natural scent similar to citronella, and tends to repel mosquitoes. Oregano also deters most pests.
- Grow plants that attract ladybugs. Many umbrella-shaped plants and flowers such as cilantro and scented geraniums attract ladybugs that in turn eat hungry and harmful aphids from your plants' leaves.
- Plant cucumbers or spread cucumber peels around your garden. Many insects such as ants, flies, and moths can't stand cucumbers.
- Plant spearmint or peppermint around your house or in your garden. Not only will they keep aphids away, but they also smell refreshing.

If you do find your tomatoes tormented with hornworms, check their backs to see if a parasitic wasp has developed from inside them. The larvae of the wasp emerge from inside the worm, form dozens of cocoons, and then when they hatch, they destroy the hornworm. These wasps will then patrol your garden for other feasts, so try to keep them around.

Another issue in the garden is the dreaded weed. Although some weeds are harmless and innocent in their quest for equality in your garden, they are nowhere near as appealing as your beloved flower friends and plants. The easiest option for killing weeds is to spray your garden. But, you don't have to spray harmful chemicals that could damage your soil and potentially make their way to your belly. There are other options:

- *Grip and strip*. The greenest way to get rid of weeds is to get down on your hands and knees and pull them out yourself. Pulling weeds may seem tedious to some, but if your garden isn't enormous, it can be rewarding, healthy, contemplative, and surprisingly quick. Put on your trusty gardening gloves, put on your favorite tunes, and spend some quality one-on-one time with your favorite green friends.

- *Use the news*. Line your garden with old newspapers to create a barrier for weeds. Not only are you reusing and recycling the newspaper in creative and effective ways, you are also making sure that your plants (especially your edible ones) are not getting sprayed with harmful chemicals.

- *Go bold*. Try using white vinegar as a natural weed killer. Spray it directly on the weeds in your flower or vegetable garden, or give bothersome patio pests a squirt as well.

- *Spray green*. If you want to avoid experimenting with natural remedies, then you can always try one of the countless varieties of organic sprays available at local stores, nurseries, or even online. Spraying with organic sprays will ensure that your plants aren't taking toxic breaths, and neither are you.

There are many natural ways to keep pests out of your garden. Take the time to get to know your backyard ecosystem as well as your friendly bugs and spiders. However you choose to approach your pests, just try not to give in and reach for the first can of chemical spray.

8. Pile It Up

Let's talk some trash. How many kitchen trash bags do you go through a day? How many trips do you make to the trash can while cooking? How much land do we have left to turn into enormous trash receptacles? How many of us really want to live next to one? These are some of the lingering questions surrounding us concerning our growing and expanding landfills. Garbage isn't a fun topic. When we imagine the landscape of this great and diverse country, we think of rolling hills, beautiful horizons, amber waves of grain, fruited plains—not mounting heaps of decaying waste. The amount of trash we are putting into landfills is placing our gorgeous landscape in jeopardy. And while landfills are necessary, isn't there a way we can dispose of our trash without being so trashy?

One of the greenest ways to reduce your garbage output and increase your earth input is to create, and use, a compost pile. Maybe making a compost pile isn't really the first item on your to-do list during your summer vacation, but if you take just a moment to look at the benefits of composting, you may find that trashing a small corner in your backyard could be more advantageous than you think.

First things first. What exactly is a compost pile? For those who don't specialize in trash or the decomposition of it, here's the simple answer: A compost pile is, for all practical purposes, a pile of natural and "earth healthy" trash set aside in your backyard or a small patch of grass, to be rained on, sunned, eaten by worms, and the results can later be reused for mulch or fertilizer.

Now, setting up a compost pile doesn't mean throwing all of your trash out onto your lawn and waiting for some magical trash fairy to convert it into rich and luxurious fertilizer. But the benefits of a compost pile far outweigh the negative aspects.

Getting a compost pile started is often a daunting task, but it doesn't have to be scary or intimidating. And, you don't have to travel far and wide to gather special composting tools. The most basic rule of composting is that everything is about trial and error. All you need to begin composting are kitchen scraps and yard waste. Once you have a balanced ratio of nitrogen-rich materials (or "greens" like kitchen scraps or grass clippings) and carbon-rich materials (or "browns" like dried leaves and wood chips), all you have to do is maintain it, add to it, and reap the rewards of the rich fertilizer.

Are you ready to start composting? Think of it as making a trash pie:

1. Create a small area in the corner of your yard and designate it the "crust" of the compost pile. Layer the crust of your compost pile with lawn scraps like chopped dried leaves and wood chips.

2. Add kitchen scraps. Create a layer of things like egg shells, tomato pieces, potato peels, apple cores, banana peels, or crushed walnut shells. You can use nearly anything from your kitchen counter, but you may want to avoid things like leftover meat or dairy products because they can create a pretty nasty smell. Especially in the summer. They also take longer to decompose.

3. Garnish the top of your trash pie with a little extra grass and wood chips. Make sure to completely cover the kitchen scraps to avoid unwanted pests. Drum roll, please. You are now the proud owner of a compost pile.

The majority of the kitchen scraps that hit your trash bin can be used in your compost pile. Keep a plastic container on your kitchen counter to collect "food" for your compost pile, and when you make your next salad, peel your ripe banana, or skin your cucumber, drop the scraps and trimmings that you would usually throw away into the container. You can even drop coffee grounds into the mix. Just keep a lid on the container to dissuade unwanted pests from feasting. Egg shells are fantastic where composting is concerned; just make sure to crush the shells so they will easily decompose.

Now that your trash pie has all the ingredients, sit back and let nature take over. Although a compost pile is one of the easiest and best ways to fertilize your garden, it does need a little tender loving care to make sure that all is well. Basically, just rotate it to aerate it every now and then, moving the top layer to the bottom and vice versa. The easiest way to ensure that your compost is "moving" is to rotate it every time you add something to it. Also, make sure to check the temperature of your compost pile. If it feels warm, all is well. However, if it isn't warm to the touch, you may need to add more nitrogen (green) materials. If you want compost fairly quickly, chop or shred the materials to keep the process moving. Keeping yourself involved in the process could produce lush results as quickly as four weeks. You will know that your compost is ready to add to your garden soil when it is dark brown, only small bits of leaves or other materials remain, and it is crumbly. If you don't tend your compost pile, it will still work, but it may take a couple of years to produce any useable fertilizer. The key to creating a compost pile is the willingness to try.

It is fascinating to watch the whole composting process, and your plants will appreciate the fine food as well. Trash is not a fun topic, but it is always better to respect, reuse, and recycle rather than waste, disregard, and pollute. Just look at it as one small way of giving back to the soil and plants that provide for you on a daily basis.

Great Green Tip

When you plant a garden, you should take the time to really get to know a gardener's best friend: mulch. Whether you buy mulch, collect it, or create it, putting mulch in your garden is one of the best ways to ensure plentiful and flowering rewards. Along with providing beautiful landscape, mulch will help retain water for your garden, prevent weeds, control the temperature of the soil, and deter unwanted pests. So, before you get to gardening, make fast friends with a fresh mound of mulch.

9. Plant a Tree

Or plant four. It is just that simple. According to a new report from the Food and Agriculture Organization (FAO) of the United Nations, roughly 32 million acres (13 million hectares) of the world's forests are cut down every year for various purposes, both private and commercial.

How many millions of acres need to be cut before we realize we are taking more than we are planting?

Although this number is alarming, the net tree loss is decreasing through replanting programs. It also has to be mentioned that, in order to live in today's society, some trees have to be cut. We do need paper and, of course, we do need homes. Lumber is always necessary. We don't have to stop cutting trees. We just need to start thinking about the long-term effects of doing so. But you don't have to travel to an endangered rainforest and chain yourself to a tree to make a difference. Change is simple and completely possible within our own backyards.

We all know that trees provide beauty, color, scenery, and shade. But trees are also the unsung heroes of our environment. Just to give them some due credit, here is a small excerpt, courtesy of the Maryland Department of Natural Resources, from the tree family's resume:

- Trees help trap pollutants such as dust, pollen, and smoke that could cause significant damage to human lungs.
- Per acre, trees produce enough oxygen to help 18 people breathe every day.
- Over a year's time, trees will have absorbed enough carbon dioxide per acre to equal the amount of carbon dioxide you produce after driving 26,000 miles.
- Trees offer shade and ecosystems for countless birds, animals, and other organisms.
- Trees have healing powers. Willow trees produce aspirin, and yew trees provide useful drugs for treating cancer.

It's okay if you want to go hug a tree now. We understand, and they definitely deserve it.

Better yet, why not do something simple, inexpensive, useful for your backyard, and necessary for the development of your ecosystem and potentially your immune system? Plant a tree today. If you are intimidated by the decision of where in your yard you should plant a tree, contact your local parks and recreation office. Or you can call your county cooperative extension office. Someone is always available to answer these questions.

If you have no backyard, or you have no more room, ask your neighbors to plant a tree. If you live in the concrete jungle, get involved with a community garden or contact your local neighborhood park and ask if you can donate money to plant trees. There is always a tree waiting to be planted and always a place to put it. With 32 million acres being cut every year, it is impossible to say there is nowhere available to plant a new life.

Planting a tree may seem like a small gesture. It may take years to really see your tree come to fruition. But you will have taken a very important step in ensuring that the next generation will have cleaner air, beautiful scenery, and a wonderful, natural jungle gym to entertain them.

Great Green Tip

Need a new way to reuse that two-liter soda bottle? Take it outside! Fill it with water, dig a small hole next to your tree, turn it upside down, and pop that bottle mouth into the soil. This will allow direct watering to the roots of your tree. If you would rather not remove, fill, and re-stick the bottle each time, cut off the bottom and use it as a funnel straight to your roots. Just make sure not to leave standing water to attract unwanted pests. You can also poke pinholes into the two-liter bottle, bury it up to the mouth in your garden, and fill it to irrigate your plants and vegetables from the roots up. Or, if you want to have some fun bird-watching time, poke a few holes in the two-liter bottle, fill it with seed, and sit it out for your extended winged family!

10. Recycle Rain

There is nothing better than a really good thunderstorm. The smell of the incoming storm. The sound of the pouring rain. The drip, drip, drip of the water falling from the gutters. Wait a sec! That water is flowing, natural, untreated, and free!

The next time the forecast calls for rain in your area, put a few buckets beneath your gutter drain or in your yard and collect it. Store it in empty milk containers or empty soda bottles or in anything that will hold it. Once you've collected it, make sure to cap the container to keep dirt and insects away from it. You can treat this water in order to use it for drinking water, but we are suggesting more fundamental uses for your water collection:

- Use that stored water for your houseplants.
- Water your hedges or bushes between rain showers.
- Wash your car or truck.
- Water your garden.
- Fill your birdbath.
- Use it for craft times outside with the kids! Mix a few drops of food coloring into some rainwater, put it in a spray bottle, and let your kids create some painting masterpieces!

The most important thing to realize is that we don't have to pay for every drop of water we use. And, we don't have to turn on our faucets and leave them running for things that nature can help us with. Collect that natural, free, and plentiful water next time it rains and watch your water bill numbers shrink while your bank account expands.

11. Recycle Your Memories

We all have a hodgepodge room in our homes. Maybe it isn't a room, but a drawer, or a closet full of treasured items that you just can't bear to throw out. Perhaps it is a broken piece of your grandmother's china. Or your grandfather's broken money clip. Or, maybe it is the first piece of pottery that your child crafted with his own hands, then cried when he broke it into hundreds of pieces. We all have treasured sentiments tied up, waiting to emerge again. But how? Why not give them new life by using them to decorate and beautify your yard?

Take an old dining room chair, for example. Most of us have an old broken chair hiding in the corner should company decide to pop in. Use it instead to create a unique, planting centerpiece.

Here's what you need:

Wooden chair
Pliers
Handsaw
Paintbrush (if desired)
Paint (if needed)
Plant

1. Knock or cut or even unscrew the legs off of the chair. You want to be able to place it directly on the ground to keep it stable and to allow plants to possibly grow through it.
2. Take off the upholstery, if there is any, using the pliers to remove tacks or upholstery staples, and use the handsaw to cut a ring into the wooden seat. Make sure that the hole is large enough to hold a pot. Or, if you would like, you can actu-

ally plant the greenery directly in the ground. Ferns are a great choice for this.

3. Decorate it. Paint it. Make it your own conversation piece.
4. Use pretty climbing plants, such as ivy or morning glory, and train them to grow up the chair spindles.
5. Place the chair anywhere you like—in your flower garden, or even on your deck.

You don't have to stop with your old furniture; you can also use smaller items like broken earrings or old costume jewelry to make beautiful stepping stones for your garden.

Here's what you need:

Pie pan, plastic planter saucers, or old cake pan
Cooking spray
Cement
Household decorative pieces

1. Choose a mold. The best mold to use when dealing with cement is a plastic planter saucer. It will easily release the cement once dried. Food boxes that can be easily torn away, like pizza boxes, also work well. You can also use an old pie pan or cake pan to act as a mold to hold the cement. Just make sure to liberally coat the bottom of any mold chosen with cooking spray to allow the cement to release when it hardens.
2. Mix the cement, pour it in the mold, and wait for it to slightly harden. Tap the container to make sure there are no bubbles in the cement. You may have to use paper towels to collect any excess water on top.
3. Use anything you like to make a mosaic pattern: A bro-

ken drinking glass. (Just be careful!) Old belt buckles. Unmatched buttons. Leftover aquarium rocks. You can use any kind of shiny personal items that have been hovering in your drawers, closets, or jewelry boxes for years, searching for a home.

4. Give kids a chance to get in on the fun and use their hands and feet to really personalize your garden stones. Use broken pieces of their first Christmas ornament or fragments of their baby picture frames. Use pieces of champagne glasses from your wedding day to create an anniversary stone. Or, write special dates in the cement to solidify celebration or memorial stones.

5. Allow the stones to dry, pop them out, and place them in your garden.

You can make everything from name plaques, wreaths, wind chimes, and sun catchers using items from your home. The point is to search your home for personal lawn and house decorations before you drive somewhere to buy something that may never capture your own unique family memories. You save gas, money, and energy, and you create something that is personalized and artistic. After all, the beauty of hodgepodge art is in the eye of the memory holder.

Great Green Tip

Do you love animals too much to use chemicals to keep them out of your garden? But, do you love eating your homegrown vegetables just as much as those roaming critters? Deer are some of the worst for grazing through a garden. One of the easiest and greenest ways to avoid using chemcals is to sprinkle some of your hair clippings around your garden. If that doesn't appeal to you, consider leaving your "scent" outside. You can deter hungry critters by leaving urine around your garden. If you don't feel like collecting and spreading your own personal "scent," allow your pet to do that dirty work for you!

PART TWO
Bring It Home

Simple, affordable green tips from your kitchen pantry to your attic space.

Now that you have a few simple green tricks for your backyard, we'll take you through a room-by-room tour of your house, pointing out easy ways to live greener and still save money. Each room contains distinct green possibilities, from naturally lighting your living room to setting up your own clothing exchange from your bedroom closet. We will show you how to give new life to your collection of unpaired socks, and how to create your own toilet cleaner.

It can be overwhelming to consider giving your home a green makeover. After all, if it isn't broken, why fix it? Sure, your home is undeniably yours, and you have worked hard to craft it into a personal refuge from the world. However, if you take the time to get a haircut, wash your clothes, clean your car, or even make your bed, why not take some time to "manicure" your home? Especially if it means adding money back into your bank account. Make your way to the most comfortable room in your home, settle into your favorite reading chair, and read on to find simple and affordable ways to give your home a green makeover.

Your Kitchen: Add a Little Green to Your Diet

12. Develop Your Kitchen's Ecosystem

Feeding a family can be daunting. Feeding any family is hard whether there be two, four, or twenty-four. Buying food, growing food, cooking food, or wasting food, it all eventually adds up both in your pocketbook or wallet and in your energy output.

The kitchen is the life center of your home, and it often functions like its own ecosystem: food undergoing its own metamorphosis from ingredients from a store or garden to a lovely, home-cooked smorgasbord of flavors. Alongside those flourishing creations, you may have hibernating species that have remained dormant for years. How many times have you pushed aside that old cereal box? How many times do you find yourself buying something you just have to have, and then watching it take up space in your pantry or fridge? We all do it. We all have food that just sounded good and then went bad.

No more. Set aside one day and make yourself go through the pantry, fridge, and freezer. Create a pile each for garbage, food you will definitely use, and food that, no matter how much you wish you could eat it, you just won't. A good rule of thumb: If it hasn't been used in five months, it isn't going to be used. Get it out.

You will be amazed with what you find, and you will begin to

35

realize just how much you have been buying for no particular reason. Throw away any food that is spoiled or past its expiration date. Arrange your fridge in the order of oldest items to newest. Go through that snack bin, and get rid of the stale crackers and old chips.

When you are finished, step back for a moment and assess your unused food items, and use the green approach to find a new use for them. Take those food items that are unopened and can still be used and donate them. Check out the food pantry at a local church, synagogue, or homeless shelter, or search your neighborhood for a fellow person who would enjoy your unused items. Just because you didn't use something doesn't mean someone else can't.

Then, take one last look at what is unsalvageable. Say goodbye to it for the last time, and attempt to stock and maintain your kitchen with only what your family will use. By using only what you need and buying only what you will eat, you are reducing the amount of waste that leaves your kitchen and you are putting more money back into your bank account. Take the time to really tend to your kitchen and to allow for only those ingredients that keep you happy, healthy, and sustained. Doing so will cause your kitchen environment to grow and prosper, allowing you to reap a fruitful harvest from your pantry.

13. If It's Not on a List, It Doesn't Exist

Now that you have taken the time to purge your kitchen, it is time to stock it with only the necessary items needed for cooking. How many times have you come from the grocery store amazed by how much you have needlessly bought? Those days are over!

Before you head out on your next grocery shopping trip, take inventory of your food and decide what you truly need. Avoid impulse-buy items arranged at kid-level, or at eye-level, while waiting in the checkout line.

The easiest way to avoid overbuying at the store is to make a menu. Before you go to the grocery store, take the time to map out your dinners for the week. Get the family involved, and decide which night is spaghetti night, and which night will require the most work. Get everyone's schedule for the week, and plan your meals accordingly. Once you have your menus mapped out, make a list.

Put on your list only what you need to make your meals. Nothing more. Go through your pantry, fridge, garage, and bathrooms to decide what is absolutely necessary, and make a firm decision not to deviate once you walk the aisles. The "I can always use more" mentality leads only to waste and frivolous spending. The greener approach to shopping includes shrewdness and focus. Buy only what you need. That is one of the most important aspects of greener living. It is so important, we'll say it again. *Buy only what you need.* Write it at the top of the list to remind yourself. Say it over and over again, like a mantra, while perusing the supermarket aisles.

That said, everyone needs a little wiggle room, so go ahead and allow for some splurge items. Create a set amount of extras for each person in the family. Stick to it, though. If you decide that each child can pick out only one special snack for the week, don't deviate. Keeping yourself and the rest of the family in check while shopping is one of the easiest ways to avoid excess waste.

Speaking of waste, let's take a second to discuss buying in bulk. The price club stores that are out there only encourage our desires to always have bigger and better. Sure, they do have their place. Buying in bulk can be a good thing if you need to stock up through winter, or if you have a large family to feed. You have to find a way to cut corners when necessary. However, buying a box of 200 burritos because you just love them isn't really saving you money. By the time you are through your 101st burrito, hating the thought of ever cooking another, how long will the other 99 burritos sit frozen, untouched, wasted, and taking up needed space? Before you give in to the urge to have more, take the time to really understand your family's needs, and then buy accordingly.

Once you learn to shop for what you truly need, you can put away your groceries with the pride that you have succeeded in making your shopping a greener experience, providing excellent and well-planned meals, using only what you need and buying only what you use. The best way to keep your money in the bank and your shopping green is to just keep it simple.

14. It's in the Bag

So you finished your weekly menu and shopping list, bought only the items on that list, and now you stand at the end of the checkout line at the supermarket, faced with yet another choice: paper or plastic. There are so many benefits in going with plastic: Easier handholds. Less tearing. Fewer trips from the car to the house. Although these are all valid reasons for convenience, is plastic really the better choice?

The argument of paper versus plastic is ongoing and convoluted. Although many stores have made the decision to move to a more eco-friendly plastic bag, and plastic bags take up relatively small spaces when compacted in a landfill, we stand by paper bags as the greener way to go when it comes to easier and consistent recycling. Nearly every recycling center will take paper bags. Not all recycle plastic bags. And plastic is starting to lose its luster. For example San Francisco has become the first city in the United States to ban the use of plastic bags at large supermarkets and pharmacies.

But that doesn't mean plastic isn't the more convenient option. Who hasn't attempted to lift the heavy paper bag of groceries from the car, dangling purse, briefcase, or child in one hand, pinching key ring in the other, only to have that recyclable and biodegradable paper bag rip and spill your precious groceries all over the concrete? It happens. And it isn't fun. But, given that choosing paper really does make a difference both in prices at the grocery store and in the environment, maybe it is worth the effort to choose paper and make one more trip to the car. Especially since Americans go through and throw away 100 billion plastic bags every year. It takes 12 million barrels of oil to manufacture that many bags.

If the thought of paper just really puts you off, consider reusing some of those plastic bags in other ways. Since plastic bags are one of the most littered pieces of trash in our world, here are a few simple and green ways to make a difference:

- Pack your lunch in one.
- Change the cat litter with a used grocery bag.
- Pick up after the puppy when you walk him.
- Line your bathroom trash can with one.
- Use them as trash bags in your vehicle.
- Return them to your supermarket for recycling.

Many stores now have large green recycling bins at the front of the store in order to encourage shoppers to recycle their plastic bags. So the next time you need to go to the store, gather all the plastic bags from your previous trip and take them back. It is easy and effortless to drop them off on your way in.

Another greener possibility with plastic is to decline the "double bag" option. Yes, milk is heavy, and double bagging offers you a temporary convenience, but the tradeoff is that you're left with a virtually unused second plastic bag. If you absolutely need a double bagged item, then make sure to reuse that bag in some way so that its mere existence hasn't been wasteful and in vain.

There's another plastic bag villain lurking in the fruit and vegetable section of your grocery store—plastic bags stashed next to the produce. Sure, they're convenient for keeping your tomatoes together and your green onions from falling through the cracks of your cart. But the one thing we all need to remember about fruits and vegetables is that they travel for miles in a box without these plastic bags. They sit in displays without the plastic bags. They also have this little miraculous "skin" that keeps them from just melting and disintegrating in your cart. You can shop with your fruits and vegetables just cruising in your cart with no plastic bag to protect them. It may seem scary, but once you try it, you will begin to wonder who decided that we all needed the little fruit and vegetable plastic bags to begin with. That is a conspiracy theory worth checking out!

If you're still torn between paper and plastic, then skip both options and consider taking your own cloth bag into the store. Yes, sometimes the cashiers do look at you and your cool little cloth bag with arched eyebrows, but think of it this way: you're a trendsetter! Choosing to use and reuse a cloth bag to shop is the greenest option available. Especially when it is made from organic cotton, or if you're able to use tote bags you already had at home.

Let's face it, plastic is convenient. But if you choose it, make sure to reuse it. And know that when you make the conscious choice to use and recycle a paper bag rather than choosing a plastic bag, you are doing your part to help decrease the 100 billion bags currently sitting in landfills and littering our beautiful parks. Finally, don't be afraid to be a trendsetter. Next time you're at the neighborhood supermarket, whip out your canvas bag with pride!

Great Green Tip

Try going out to eat only once a month. When you really take the time to make it special, it becomes a treat and a family event rather than a routine. And, you will be making a greener choice by choosing to stay home more often, using what you already have available in your own pantry, not driving and wasting gas, and avoiding excess. Think about the leftovers from that appetizer you often order. Where does it go when you are finished with it? What about the bread that comes to your table? When you only choose one roll from the overflowing basket, what happens to the other rolls when they are taken away? They are thrown out. They cannot be served again. What about the paper napkins, straw wrappers, and disposable cups? You got it: trash! Instead, ask for only the amount you will eat, and share your appetizers or entrees to ensure they are all eaten. Skip the straw or the disposable plastic lid, if you feel comfortable doing so. Make going out to eat an event that is anticipated, well thought out, and completely enjoyed.

15. Buy "Ourganically"

With green choices becoming trendy and sometimes adding extra expenses, it is often hard to know which way to turn in the green world. Take organic food, for instance. Who doesn't want to eat more healthily, to avoid pesticides and scary preservatives?

With so many choices at the grocery store, we all need a little
jump-start here and there when it comes to the nutritional value
of the food we put in our mouths. However, is buying organically
the easiest and greenest option available? When you do make the
choice between traditional farming and organic farming, are you
frustrated with the price at the checkout? There are ways to avoid
it. And one of those include buying "ourganically"(what is local
and best for *you*). You can still make healthy, green choices without breaking your piggy bank. So, when you're planning your next
grocery list, ask yourself: What difference does organic food make?

One of the hottest discussions in the green debate is whether
or not organic food is proven to be better for us or for the environment. It is hard to say, thus far, whether organic is truly better
in all areas of eating and farming. And, according to the AgBioWorld
website, it may be impossible to consider organic farming as an adequate food supply for the world. More land is needed for cows
to produce more manure to create more compost to feed the organic crops. Therefore, more land has to be cleared and trees chopped
down in order to accommodate the organic demands. Now, this
may not seem relevant when discussing health issues, but consider
how many species can or will be displaced in order to make more
room for and to cultivate organic farms.

However, there's no doubt that the pesticides commonly used
on fresh fruits and vegetables are not healthy for us. According to
the Natural Resources Defense Council website, the use of pesticides in farming is suspected of increasing cancer and reproductive
issues in humans. Additionally, the National Academy of Sciences
has classified more than 80 percent of common pesticides as possible carcinogens. Those figures alone are enough to argue for organic food as a healthy alternative. But, which is the better payoff?
Clearing more land, which could harm our already fragile ecosystem, or using potentially harmful chemicals? Quite the quandary,

isn't it? As Isaac Newton aptly put it, reactions will always follow actions. And those good intentions can often garner harmful results. So, which is the best "ourganic" green choice for you?

For starters, let's define what it means to "buy organic." Organic food is grown, processed, harvested, or combined naturally. That means no artificial preservatives are added to stored or canned food, and no chemicals are used when growing fruits or vegetables. The methods used are still being studied and created as we speak. Many organic farmers are developing new methods of using composting materials as well as bringing in helpful insects and critters to take the place of once widely used insecticides and chemicals. The problem is that growing organic food often requires more experimentation, more land and "fertilizing" cattle, and more work. All of that adds up to potentially healthier food—but higher prices at the supermarket.

With prices rising in nearly every aspect of our lives, is it necessary to buy everything organic? The simple answer is no. The green answer is to buy "ourganically." Pick and choose where you feel an organic option is healthiest and greenest for you. If your family eats a lot of fruits and vegetables, then buy the organic variety. If you prefer that artificial preservatives not be allowed in your house, then buy organic canned food. The simple solution to a trendy, and pricey, organic way of life is to create an "ourganic" way of life and buy what you will use and what you can afford. If you can't afford it, and you want to eat organically, then consider cutting back on other splurge items. Making healthy, organic options a priority often creates a way to afford it. Better yet, scrap paying for them, and go even more "ourganic" by growing your own!

Buying organic is a personal choice and arguably one that, in terms of the scope of agribusiness in the United States, isn't going to have a significant environmental impact. However, you can make a significant, environmental, "ourganic" impact at the local level by buying seasonally and from your local farmers. When you buy fruits or vegetables that aren't in season, they have to be transported from a region or area suitable for growing them. Transporting requires gas. Big trucks create more pollution. Buy fruits or vegetables that are in season for your area, and buy locally when you can. The closer the food is grown to you, the fewer miles and dollars required to deliver it.

Buying "ourganically" can mean buying from local farmers' markets (which not only supports your local farmers but also decreases the storage time your food spends in a mass market waiting to be picked up) or actually going to a farm to pick and choose for yourself. Orchards and farms are usually open to allowing the public in to pick fruits and vegetables, and encourage you to spend time understanding and participating in the farming culture in your area.

The one key to buying "ourganically" is to buy what you will use, what you will need, and what is most important to you. Finding the perfect balance for you and your family is what will make buying organically and/or locally a lifestyle choice rather than a trend. If you do choose organic, just make sure to eat it before it goes to waste. Without those chemicals and preservatives that we are all used to, the shelf life of organic food is often cut in half. If you think about it, should a banana really last more than a few days? Take the time to think about why you would choose to buy organic food, then buy only what fits into your family's "ourganic" lifestyle. You can decrease pollution, save energy and gas, and support your local growing community by buying locally. That's the green and simple way to make a difference.

16. Spice It Up

Whether it is the sage in your Thanksgiving stuffing, the cilantro in your fresh-made salsa, or the cinnamon bursting from a hot, moist cinnamon roll, the intoxicating aromas of herbs and spices can't be beat. If just thinking of those aromas makes your mouth water, then consider growing your own herbs in order to keep your taste buds happy.

One of the easiest ways to reduce your costs and increase the green pigment in your thumb is to grow your own ingredients. You don't need a perfect patch of grass, and you don't have to worry about neighborhood animals hopping over to your house for a snack. All you need to grow your own herbs (considered a leafy plant) or spices (obtained from seeds, roots, or bark, although some argue spices are created from herbs) is a pot and a window.

Making a window herb garden is easy, fun, and cost and eco-efficient. All you need are seeds, pots, sun, water, and the taste buds to drive you. Plant your seeds just as you would for any other houseplant or bulb. Love them. Water them. Nurture them. And then cut them and eat them. It is just that easy. Once you grow the herbs, you can also hang them and dry them to use at a later date. You can cut them or grind them in a coffee grinder, and then store them in old spice containers or baby food jars.

The best way to plan your window garden is to pay attention to what you cook. Take the time to notice which herbs or spices you always reach for and what flavors catch your nose at the grocery store. Once you have herbs at your fingertips, you will begin to search for a chance to pluck and eat them. What better way to put that fresh cilantro to use than through pairing it with fresh tomatoes, garlic, and even jalapeño peppers from your own green thumb?

Fresh Salsa

4 fresh tomatoes from your garden
½ cup chopped red or white onion
2 tablespoons fresh chopped cilantro from your window garden
1 finely chopped jalapeño or serrano pepper
Squeezed juice from one lime
½ teaspoon salt
½ teaspoon minced garlic

Chop the tomatoes and combine all ingredients. You can choose to sauté your onions to bring out their flavor, or leave them freshly chopped for extra crunch. Make sure to remove the seeds and core from the pepper if you wish for a mild salsa. You can finely chop the ingredients for a thicker, chunkier salsa, or you can throw it all in the food processor for smoother texture.

Growing green, leafy friends isn't for everybody. But eating is. The next time you find yourself reaching for an herb or spice, make the decision to plant it instead. Let your taste buds guide you. Once you have tasted the fabulous flavors of your own herbs and spices, you won't want to go back to buying them. Plus you will be making a very important decision in the process of going green: If you grow your own herbs, you will be eating organically, saving money, gas, and energy, and making a difference in this world. Even if it is just one herb at a time.

Great Green Tip

Is your trash or recycling bin overflowing with empty yogurt containers? Try reusing them for your fledgling plants. Cut a drainage hole in the bottom, place a plastic lid under it, and plant your seeds. Why buy a new seedling pot when you can make your own? You can also reuse egg containers or empty Chinese food containers as well. Before you toss or recycle that empty container, search your green brain for new ways to reuse it. Your plants will thank you!

17. Dine and Dab with Cloth

Family time at the dinner table can fall by the wayside if you're always on the go. On a typical night, a dash through the drive-thru or dinner on the run might be the norm for you, rather than the exception. But, when you do have time to sit as a family and eat, take the time to really make it special.

Why not take dinner from mundane to memorable—and save the Earth at the same time? Shelve the paper napkins and paper towels. Instead, pull out your cloth napkins. Put decorative rings around them. Fold them into fun animal shapes. If you care enough about your family to cook five-star dinners, then shouldn't your efforts be treated with five-star respect? And don't stop with your cloth napkins—use real silverware. Use your china, or break out the crystal. Make your table the one place where you don't rush, skimp, or cheat yourself or your family out of a great experience. Make your dinners an occasion.

If you just can't bear the thought of parting with your paper towels or napkins, try to buy recycled products. According to the Natural Resources Defense Council website, if every American household replaced one roll of regular paper towels with 100 percent recycled paper towels, 544,000 trees could be saved. And if every American household replaced one package of paper napkins with 100 percent recycled ones, 1 million trees could be saved. Think of how many trees you could save if no paper is ever purchased for wiping your mouth.

When you are finished, throw them in the wash with your already dirty bath towels, then use them again and again.

Even if you only use cloth napkins once a week, you are making a difference in the amount of waste you produce. There's little effort involved in switching to cloth napkins, and your family will appreciate the change. Who doesn't want to feel special at mealtime? We all deserve it, even if it is just a small change.

Great Green Tip

Looking for simple and effective ways to conserve water in your kitchen? Try using the same drinking glass throughout the day. Why drink from a glass, put it in the dishwasher, and then get out a new one when you get thirsty again? After all, only *your* lips have touched it. Reuse it and save that water and energy you would otherwise use to wash it. Also, if you are a coffee or tea drinker, and you are only indulging in one cup, use only enough water to make what you will drink. Taking the time to make smarter consumption decisions will ultimately make a significant impact in water conservation as well as your wallet!

18. Doctor Your Fridge and Freezer

You have purged your house of unnecessary food. You have cleaned out your pantry, made a menu of weekly meals, made a list, and stuck to it while shopping at the grocery store. You are skipping the plastic bags and opting for paper or cloth instead. You are on your way to a clutter-free and green kitchen!

Your next step in keeping your food happy and healthy is to check out your freezer and refrigerator.

If left unmanaged, a lot of energy can be wasted:

1. *Take your fridge's temperature.* If you have your temperature set to 32°F or below, then your money is flowing straight out of your pocket and into the electric company's. Most refrigerators come with an adjustable temperature setting. According to the U.S. Department of Energy, your fridge should be kept between 37 and 40°F. Any higher and your food could begin to create dangerous bacteria, and we don't want that. Any lower you are only using excess energy and taking your hard-earned money from your pocket. Keeping tabs on the temperature will prevent throwing away your money and frozen, spoiled food.

2. *Don't overstuff your fridge.* Keeping your fridge stocked with only items you will use rather than one too many will keep the air flow properly circulating, which in turn keeps your energy use in check.

3. *Cover up.* Make sure to always cover leftover food when you store it. Not only does it keep your fridge from smelling like last night's dinner, but also, according to the U.S. Department of Energy, uncovered food increases moisture within your fridge, which in turn makes it work harder.

4. *Seal it tight.* Make sure your fridge door completely closes to prevent the escape of cold air. You don't want your fridge working overtime to cool your entire kitchen.

5. *Avoid cold chills.* Make sure to defrost your freezer regularly to keep the air circulating properly. According to the U.S. Department of Energy, any more than ¼ inch buildup of frost could increase your energy bill.

6. *Keep it cool.* According to the U.S. Department of Energy,

your freezer should be kept at 5°F, or 0°F if you have a stand-alone freezer for long-term storage. This is a safe temperature for your food, and you can also avoid that "frozen block" syndrome when it is time to pull a frozen dinner from your freezer.

Keeping your freezer and refrigerator in proper working order and set to the proper temperature will decrease your energy use and increase your pocket change. After all, who wants to give more money to your electric company when you can use the extra cash to eat like a king!

19. Ditch Disposable Dishes

According to the U.S. EPA, 25,000,000,000 foam cups are thrown away every year. Yes, that does say 25 *billion*. In America alone. And that number doesn't include plates and bowls. The foam cup that could be in your hand today will still be sitting in a landfill somewhere 500 years from now. Those are amazing statistics.

Disposable is easier. But it is definitely not greener.

Coffee to go is one of the main culprits here. There are recyclable options out there, and there are places that offer paper cups rather than foam (which is better, but still wasteful), but the best green option is to use your own handy, stainless-steel, never-has-to-leave-your-side travel mug. Before you leave for work each morning, set your trusty mug next to your keys. Fill it with homebrew before you leave, or stop at your favorite coffee haunt on the way and tell your server that you have your own container. Some servers may be confused, but most of them understand and happily oblige.

If you're used to getting your morning brew at a gas station, you're in luck. Most gas stations will comply and charge a lot less if you use your own mug. But some will still charge the same exact price. Although most gas stations have encountered the mug-toter, you still may come across a confused and resistant cashier along the way. But a simple explanation of your desire to save your environment as well as the environment of the person questioning you often settles any ill will about not using the store-supplied foam cup.

With foam cups galore in our country, it only seems natural to pair them with disposable dinnerware. Foam plates, while often handy and convenient, are environmentally the worst possible option for serving food within your own home. They will hold hot food. They do not cave like paper plates under a heavy load of casserole. They are easy to throw away, and there is no washing involved. Easy is nice. However, those nice, easy, disposable foam plates will far outlast you, your children, your grandchildren, your great-grandchildren, and so on. Rather than buy foam and then just throw it away, why not use and reuse your real, nondisposable, sturdy dishes? What good are your perfectly nice dishes doing you just sitting in a cupboard, hiding behind a door? Dishes are for putting food on and for eating from. Although your dishes are reliable, green, and suited to your personal taste, using your everyday dishes may pose a problem for situations like camping or fun picnicking. However, there are options out there to help you avoid the foam trap. When you are choosing to take your meals into the lovely outdoors in order to enjoy all that natural ambiance, skip the disposable dishes and buy hard plastic or reusable camping dishes. You will still have to wash them while camping or you will have to bring dirty dishes back to your house in your handy picnic basket. However, making the choice to use and reuse your outdoor dishes avoids breaking your real ones, and also keeps that sneaky foam from stowing away and hitching a ride.

Just make sure not to throw them away. It isn't fun to have to bring home dirty dishes after a fun day out, but making the decision to throw them away only adds more trash to our landfills. Besides, if you bring them home and wash them, they are there for your next outdoor adventure.

If you just don't want to use the dishes in your cabinets, and paper plates will not hold your piping hot lasagna, then you do have an option. Recycle your foam. Not all recycling centers recycle the various types of polystyrene, but if your plate, cup, bowl, leftover container, or coffee mug has a number 6 on the bottom, it is more commonly accepted. Since not all recycling centers take foam, you do have one more option: You can mail it in. Go to the website www.epspackaging.org/info.html. For a small fee, you can mail in your used, rinsed foam and they will provide a recycling service for you. Or you can visit earth911.org/ and search for a recycling center that accepts foam. It will allow you to search within a 100 mile radius. Yes, that is quite the hassle.

So why not just avoid foam altogether? You have lovely pieces of china and fantastic dinnerware and goblets waiting and begging to be held and caressed. Use your dishes. That is what they are for. And think about the money you are saving by using and reusing what you already have. Isn't that better than literally throwing your money and your dinnerware in the trash?

20. Sit Back and Get Lazy

There is nothing better than a hearty meal and a full belly. Your mind drifts to images of decadent desserts, or to the couch in the living room that seems to be beckoning you with plush pillows and a comfortable throw. You push yourself from the table, stretch your arms in contentment, and look over your shoulder to find piles and piles of spattered and sauce-caked dirty dishes.

Ah, the joy of cleaning dishes. Many families dine from paper or foam plates in order to avoid the pain and agony of scrubbing dirty dishes. Sure, it is more convenient, but considering that an average American family of four dines three times a day from foam or paper plates (and let's not forget that paper plates often have to be doubled in order to uphold the weight of the food), that is a *minimum* of twelve plates hitting the trash a day. And that is assuming no additional plates are used to serve dessert, as serving plates, or as snack holders throughout the rest of the day. Now, multiply that times thirty days, and you have an average family of four going through at least 360 plates a month. That equals 4,320 disposable plates a year.

Why not give your real dishes another try? Rather than wasting money and resources on disposable dishes, consider using your reusable, sturdy, never-leak-food plates and washing them with a small amount of water and soap. You will be saving money and going green at the same time. Some may say that washing dishes leads to wasting water. You do have to use water to wash, there is no way around that, but according to the American Water Works Association using your dishwasher may be the easiest and greenest way out of washing dishes:

- Depending on your brand of dishwasher, you use between 9 and 12 gallons of water a load.
- There are newer dishwashers available that can lower that number to 7 gallons of water a load. These dishwashers usually come with an ENERGY STAR label stating that they have been governmentally approved, through the U.S. EPA guidelines, to save energy.
- Hand washing often uses as much as 20 gallons of water.

Considering that many of us only use our dishwasher once a day or every other day whereas you may hand wash dishes three times a day, it is more efficient and wastes less water to use your dishwasher. With newer dishwashers falling under the ENERGY STAR program, we can expect a surge of new environmentally friendly dishwashers. If you are not in the market for a new dishwasher, there are ways to conserve energy and go green with your old one.

1. *Don't pre-rinse.* One of the water traps when using a dishwasher is rinsing your dishes before you put them in. The easy way to avoid using excess water to rinse as well as elbow grease is to try a load without rinsing. Yes, you may have to scrape and wash some dishes again. But you will know the full capability of your dishwasher. And once you know whether the dishwasher can or cannot get that caked food off your dishes, then you will be able to adequately judge how much water is needed to pre-rinse. There is no need to use excess water without first finding out if it is even necessary. In many cases, especially with newer dishwashers, very little rinsing is required before running a load of dishes. Why waste more water when your dishwasher will do the dirty work?

2. *Fill 'er up!* Another way to save water and energy is to only run the dishwasher when it is completely full. Washing a few dishes uses the same amount of energy and water as running a full load. So, load up and squeeze in every dish possible. Get creative and find room for that last glass!

3. *Turn off the heat.* Although many dishwashers offer the option to heat-dry your dishes, if it is possible, turn off that option. It is nice to open a newly run dishwasher and find little to no water on your dishes. However, if you just let them sit a little longer, they will air dry, and you will save energy in the

process. Look at it this way, the longer they take to dry, the more time you have to do other things. Like lie on the couch and sleep off your meal. It is the same as letting your dishes dry in a rack, so give it a try.

4. *Go green with detergent.* If you want your dishwashing experience to be extra green, try using an eco-friendly dishwashing detergent. They are competitively priced, and they lack phosphates that often tend to journey to our oceans and waterways. According to the NRDC website, phosphates can cause oxygen depletion and excess algae growth in our waterways. Without sufficient oxygen, fish and other aquatic animals can die.

If you don't have a dishwasher, you can still save water by washing with a conservative hand. You can always hand wash by filling the sink, but it isn't necessary, and it can lead to excess waste through rinsing and refilling the sink. When you think about it, if you fill your sink—or one side if you have a double sink—to wash your dishes, by the time you reach that tenth plate, how clean is that water?

Washing your dishes with this next method saves more water than filling a sink and rinsing after each dish:

1. Scrape any excess food off the plates and into the trash. Don't allow water pressure to do what a little elbow grease can.
2. Rinse the dishes with water.
3. Turn off the water and scrub with soap and a wet cloth. Or you can use one of those handy soap-filled scrubbers.
4. Try to clean as many dishes as possible before rinsing them again.
5. Turn on the water long enough to rinse again. And try to rinse them all at the same time. If you have a double sink,

place all dishes on one side in a drying rack and rinse them together. This will avoid using water to rinse each individual dish.

The easiest and greenest way to clean your dishes just happens to be the laziest. So, go ahead and lounge on the couch. Relax, digest, and sleep while the dishwasher does all the dirty work!

Great Green Tip

Try dining by candlelight with your spouse, partner, roommate, significant other, alone, or with your kids. Take the time to relax and unwind. Or curl up with your favorite book, and allow the ambiance and the soft, flickering candles to do their thing. If you want to go that extra green mile, use soy candles to create that glow.

21. Turn It In

How much trash leaves your kitchen every day? According to an EPA study in 2006, Americans generated over 251 million tons of waste. Although nearly 82 million tons of that trash was recycled, that still left 169 million tons of waste.

The EPA also reports that we saved the energy equivalent of more than 10 billion gallons of gasoline by recycling that nearly 82 million tons of waste. That number alone can and should encourage us to keep pushing for real trash reduction in our landfills. Sure, we have all heard about recycling, and we all, for the most part, realize and believe that it is something that everyone should do. But how many of us actually do it? So, the next time you open your trash can, stop and think: Can you recycle that empty dishwasher detergent container instead of throwing it away?

If you are interested in recycling but you aren't so sure where to begin, wonder no more. If you don't have a recycling bin already, contact your garbage collection center to ask if they provide recycling services. If so, they will provide a recycling bin for pickup. If your garbage company doesn't offer recycling options, some recycling centers do offer pickup. Once you have your recycling information in hand, put a box next to your trash can to ensure that you don't forget and accidentally toss your empty peanut butter jar in with the trash. You also need to make sure to adequately clean your recyclables before adding them to your collection. That will prevent unwanted smells and pests from infiltrating your home.

If you feel a bit confused or intimidated about what can be recycled, here is a list to remove some of the guesswork:

- Milk jugs
- Juice containers
- Plastic bottles from dressings, jellies, or sauces
- Tin cans
- Cardboard boxes like cereal boxes or quickie side dish options
- Glass bottles
- Aluminum cans
- Two-liter bottles
- Dishwashing detergent or soap bottles
- Empty household cleaning bottles

This is only a short list to get you started. But, for the most part, your kitchen contains more recyclable items than any other room in your house.

One way to tell if an item is recyclable is to check the bottom of the container. Look for a symbol of three arrows forming a triangle. When dealing with plastics, the triangle should contain a number which represents a recycling code for the different types of materials. That number tells you into which recycling category your plastic trash falls. For example, most of the time, the number 2 will appear on plastic bottles for liquid detergent or juice. So that you don't overflow your kitchen with large piles of bottles, check with your local recycling center to ensure which numbers they take before you begin collecting. And to remove some of the confusion, check out www. thedailygreen.com for a more detailed list.

The only barrier to this simple process is that some states and communities do not offer curbside recycling pickup. However, don't be discouraged, recycling friends. You can still contact the recycling center closest to you and ask what containers and trash you can bring in. This does require you to actually pack the recyclables in your vehicle and take it to the recycling center. That is, admittedly, a disadvantage, but most likely something you can build into your weekly routine. You will feel better after you do, and you will be taking a very proactive step in reducing the amount of trash overflowing our landfills. Given the staggering statistics from the EPA, how can you afford *not* to recycle?

When you do recycle, you are making an important change in not only your life, but also other lives as well. One important thing to remember: If you recycle, try to also buy recycled items when possible. Some of the most commonly recycled household objects include:

- Cereal boxes or side dish options
- Paper napkins
- Stationery
- Greeting cards
- Toilet paper
- Paper towels

You don't have to break your bank buying only recycled products, but taking the time to think about what you use most and then buying the recycled version really does make a difference. If you use a lot of paper towels, buy recycled ones. They aren't as soft, but how soft should a *paper* towel be? Convenience is nice, but so is taking care of our Earth.

While it may seem intimidating, or hard to understand just how these products are reprocessed to create new things, recycling is one of the easiest and most productive ways to create positive change for not only you, but also your neighbors as well. We have already reduced our trash numbers, and think about those 10 billion gallons of energy equivalent gasoline we saved through our recycling efforts. Why not increase that? Real change is simple, accessible, and sitting there in your trash can, waiting for you to make a difference.

22. Save Your Trash's Life

Although recycling often conjures images of green bins and large recycling centers, let's not forget the simple and basic meaning of "recycle," to use again. There are countless useful ways to use and reuse several items that would normally hit your trash or recycling bin. If you can find a new way to bring life to your trash, then you are reducing the amount of waste you produce and increasing the livelihood and longevity of the planet.

Obviously, you can't make peanut butter to refill your empty jar. (Well, you could, but that is just a totally different book!) However, you can reuse those empty glass or plastic jars and butter or margarine containers for storing food rather than buying plastic storage containers. Just make sure to label them to avoid searching through fifteen butter tubs to find last night's mashed potatoes.

Also, another little reused item in the kitchen is the plastic sandwich bag. How often do we put things like granola, cereal, or sandwiches in them, use them once, and then throw them away? Why? Instead, simply flip them inside out, wash them, leave them to dry, and reuse them. It is easy and requires little to no effort to do. This method works well for bags that contain dry goods or veggies. However, you may want to just chuck the bag where raw meats are concerned.

Looking for something to do with your two-liter plastic soda bottles? Engage your kids in a fun and educational activity and use a bottle to create a terrarium.

Here's how:

1. Wash it thoroughly before you begin, and remove the label.
2. Use scissors or a knife to cut off the top quarter of the bottle and poke holes in it.
3. Layer the bottom of the bottle with 1–2 inches of pebbles for drainage. (You can add a layer of activated charcoal for filtration, but that is optional.)
4. Top the pebbles with Spanish moss to give the roots room to grow.
5. Add a heaping layer of soil. Try to use one that contains mostly humus, sand, or peat.
6. Plant your seeds in the soil just as you would in any other pot. Nearly any indoor houseplant will work. Just make sure that it doesn't have the potential or desire to bust the seams of your terrarium.
7. Water.
8. Decorate your terrarium to add a little flare. Create a theme and let your imagination run wild. Add trinkets, bells or shells to liven it up.

9. Reattach the top portion of the bottle and seal it with tape.

10. Sit back and watch the growing fun.

You will only need to water the terrarium when moisture droplets no longer appear on the top of the bottle. Buying and decorating a preassembled terrarium is fun, but why buy when you can make and participate? It is simple, productive, and educational for the kids, and it requires very little upkeep.

Another handy and versatile piece of trash is the common milk jug. One of the easiest uses for a milk jug is storing cold water in the fridge. There is nothing better than a cold glass of water, especially in the dead of summer, and what better way to use that milk jug again than to fill it with blessed H_2O?

There are several other uses for the multitasking milk jug:

- Help your kids cut off the top, poke holes in the bottom, paint it, fill it with soil and seeds, and use it for the perfect beginner's garden.
- Use it to collect that rainwater we've been talking about. Just make sure to cap it to keep pests from reproducing or making a home in it!
- Use a half-gallon milk jug to reduce water use in your toilet. (See our bathroom tips in chapter 37 for a more detailed explanation!)
- Cut off the bottom, tape the top's edges to dull them, poke holes around the mouth of the jug, and use it for a handy scooper for your kids' bathtub toys. Use the handle, scoop the toys, and store the toy-filled jug under the bathroom sink!

These ideas are only a few simple ones on a long list of options. Once you turn your sights to recycling and reusing, empty containers and potential trash will begin to leap into your inventive recycling imagination. There are hundreds of options. Before you throw out the next bag of trash, stop and rethink. Inside that kitchen trash bag are countless ways to make simple changes toward a green lifestyle.

Great Green Tip

Are you bugged by tiny bugs, fruit flies, or gnats in your kitchen? Create a natural, green cure for debugging your home. Try using a decorative bottle, or reusing a cool wine bottle, adding a small amount of apple cider vinegar and dishwashing liquid and a decorative splash like a silk flower or a handmade flower from your children to create an unnoticeable gnat trap. Insects fly in, intoxicated by the smell, and they never fly out. You will rid your kitchen of unwanted pests without spraying and with a little decorative flare!

23. Avoid the Breakfast Bag Blues

We have discussed ways to reuse your sandwich bags and plastic bags from the store, but one other reusable and very handy bag lurks in your kitchen pantry. Here's a hint: You probably have more than one variety in your cupboard. And, if you have children, the boxes probably have fruity little circles bouncing from a hearty bowl of milk. That's right: cereal box bags.

Not only are these bags handy for keeping cereal fresh, but they also have more versatility than any other bag in your kitchen. Unfortunately, this bag is rarely accepted at recycling centers, so it is often kicked to the curb with the rest of the trash. Well, not

anymore. Here are a few ways to reuse that fantastic and functional bag:

- Take it along with you when you walk your dog. Fold it
  up, put it in your back pocket, and when your dog does his
  thing, you have a poop bag all ready to go.
- Fold it up and carry it in your purse or wallet to use as a
  handy trash bag. You never know when you might need it—
  especially if your kids have a tendency to hand you sticky
  lollipop sticks.
- Take it with you to the park, and use it to pick up the litter that is bound to be there.
- Use it instead of a sandwich bag. Pack a sandwich, chips,
  granola, or crackers for a picnic.
- Stick it in your suitcase the next time you head out of town.
  You never know when you might need a divider between
  wet clothes and your business suit.
- Pack trail mix in it and take it hiking with you. When you
  are finished with it, use it for a carry-out-of-the-woods trash
  bag. Make sure to always carry out any and all trash. Even
  if you weren't the one that took it in.
- Stick it under your seat for carsick emergencies with queasy
  travelers.
- Use it for a protective table covering during craft time with
  your kids.
- Use it to crush nuts, to shake and bake, or to keep your good-
  ies separated while cooling in the fridge.
- Stick it between meat patties before you freeze them to avoid
  a frozen mess.
- Use it when scooping out your cat's litter box.
- Create a fun stained-glass project with the kids (instructions
  below).

In order to create your stained glass, you will need:

Broken crayons
Old kitchen cheese grater or sharp knife
Cereal bag
Scissors
Old towels
Iron
Yarn

1. Collect all broken and unused crayons from your house.
2. Use the cheese grater (or a knife if you prefer) to create shavings from your crayons.
3. Cut open the seams of the cereal bag and help your children cut out two mirror images of their desired design. You can leave the bag attached on one side if creating mirror images seems difficult. But cutting completely will allow more versatility in creating shapes. Just place one cutout on top of the other portion of the bag to create a mirror image.
4. Sprinkle or place the shavings on one piece of the cutout. Allow your children to create whatever designs they want. Just make sure that the shavings spread all the way to the edges of the bag to ensure that the ends stick together when you melt the shavings.
5. Place the mirror image cutout over the shavings and other cutout.
6. Cover the cereal bag with a towel.
7. Set your iron to a low temperature and gently press it into the towel, moving evenly over the entire surface. Take care not to overheat the towel or the plastic bag. Only heat it enough to make the crayon shavings melt and to seal the two pieces of cereal bag together.

8. Once the two sides are stuck together, allow it to cool. Cut a hole in the top and use the yarn to hang it from your child's window.

There are so many easy and green ways to reuse what is often an overlooked item in your kitchen. The only limit you have is your imagination. These are only a few ways to use a cereal bag, and there are hundreds of other ways you can cater to your individual lifestyle. So, before you finish that box of cereal, start thinking of new and useful ways you can reuse that bag!

Great Green Tip

When the time comes to make meals, do you often find yourself struggling to entertain your children while you chop, wash, and prepare your healthy dinner? We have the green answer to your dinnertime woes. The next time you cut that cucumber, squash, or apple, try handing a slice over to your fidgeting kids. Give them an ink pad and some paper, and cut out an image in the vegetable or fruit section. Watch them use fruit and vegetables to create stamping masterpieces while you peacefully cut, wash, and slice your way to dinner. When you are ready to eat—and they have stamped to their heart's content—throw those "stamps" into the compost container and give your trash can a break.

24. Get Off the Bottle

Having ice-cold water in the fridge is always a plus. After a long run or on a hot summer day, there is nothing like that first cold drink of water. Most of us crave it, and we all need it.

So storing it in the fridge is something that many of us do. The obvious question: bottled water or tap water?

If you are even marginally concerned about wasting water, according to the Union of Concerned Scientists, for every gallon that makes it into manufactured bottles of water, *two* gallons are wasted through the purification process. Add that to the millions of gallons of water used in the process of making the plastic. According to the Container Recycling Institute, for every 10 water bottles, 8 of those bottles wind up in a landfill or incinerator. That doesn't seem so scary or horrible, but, according to the Earth Policy Institute's website, buried bottles can take as much as one thousand years to biodegrade. One thousand years! Let's see, in the year 1008, the Crusades had not yet happened, the Magna Carta wouldn't be signed for another 207 years, and Columbus had 484 years before he sailed the ocean blue. In the year 3008, archaeologists will be searching for indications and relics of our lifestyle, and the plastic bottle will be among our artifacts. Now think about how many of those bottles you go through a week.

You can start with the obvious and choose to recycle these bottles, either by taking them to a recycling center, or by reusing them yourself. However, continuously reusing these bottles can result in harmful bacteria growth. According to the University of Minnesota Extension Food Safety website, if left at room temperature, saliva and food particles, commonly known as "backwash," in your water bottle can produce harmful bacteria. If you choose to reuse your bottle even though it is specifically designed to be a one-time-use bottle, wash it after every use with hot soapy water, and use a bottle scrubber to scrub the neck and lid. The material used to make the bottles degrades and wrinkles over time, creating tiny bacteria pockets of harmful germs. Although you may be trying to conserve by reusing that bottle, you still have to eventually throw it out. Rather than spending more money, and using more resources, and wasting excess water in order to quench your thirst, why not use the water that you are paying to have? Turn on your tap. Okay, perhaps you are concerned about the quality of your tap water. The good news is that your local water company is required to provide you with an annual water quality report. You can get one by simply contacting your water company and requesting a report. Through the EPA's "Right to Know" provisions in the Safe Drinking Water Act, each year water companies have to send out a consumer confidence report. It will give you a full breakdown of lead levels, chlorine levels and any other contaminants, and it will ease your mind as to the quality of what you are putting in your body.

Many people are rightly concerned with the amount of lead found in some tap water. As we have all seen from recent recalls, lead is a serious toxin that affects growing brains and nervous systems. You can ease those worries through your water report, or you can test your water for evidence of lead yourself. If you're interested in doing so, get more information at www.leadtesting.org. Although tap water has been given a bad rap at times, the water flowing from your faucet is actually held to higher water quality standards than most bottled water.

But if your tap does seem a bit funky, or if you can taste a slight tinge of something mysterious, you can always remedy that with a carbon filtration system. You can buy filter/pitcher combinations that both filter and hold your water, or you can connect them directly to your faucet in order to purify and drink.

Your water filter will take care of bad tastes and chlorine, copper, lead, and mercury, just to name a few. Your taste buds will thank you, and you won't return to bottled water once you take the first fabulous sip from the tap.

If all of this information still isn't enough to persuade you to break your bottle habit, consider this. According to the Public Broadcasting System (PBS), the energy we waste in using bottled water could power 190,000 homes. Imagine how "dropping the bottle" could help power homes here in the United States. And, according to the Earth Policy Institute, nearly a quarter of all bottled water is transported across international borders. Imagine how much fuel is burned just to get imported bottled water?

The Earth Policy Institute also says the most common plastic used to produce water bottles is polyethylene terephthalate (PET) which is derived from crude oil. In order to meet the annual demands for bottled water in the United States, 17 million barrels of oil must be tapped! That is enough to fuel a *million* cars in the United States for an entire year! So, the next time you fuel your car, think about that staggering statistic, and make the decision to make a change. Try your tap water.

If you are still not convinced to leave the bottle behind, then consider buying a larger jug of spring water to leave in your fridge or on your counter. They can be pricey, but when you compare them to how much you spend on a case of smaller bottled waters, they win in the long run. You can also buy a relatively inexpensive, reusable hard plastic or stainless steel bottle to take your water on the run.

Still, the easiest, greenest, and cheapest way to go is to drink water from your own faucet. And you will also give your teeth a little extra attention. The water from your faucet—that you are paying to use—also contains valuable fluoride for your teeth. That additive is not always available in the bottled water variety. And if you prefer flavored water, just squeeze a lemon into your purified, fluoride-fortified tap water, waiting for you in your reusable bottle.

25. Expose Electronic Ghosts

With oven timers buzzing, microwaves nuking, and toasters toasting, it is a constant battle keeping your electric bill in check. Everything that plugs into the wall obviously increases your bill, but what you may not know is that there are parasitic appliances that suck your electricity without you ever knowing. Sneaky little boogers!

According to the U.S. Department of Energy, home appliances and electronics are among the biggest energy using culprits, accounting for 20 percent of your energy bill. Of those energy suckers, at least 75 percent of that energy consumption occurs when electric appliances are turned off. There are several ways to stop that:

- Unplug microwaves when not in use. Anything that blinks or has a digital clock on it in your kitchen is still using energy when you are not around.
- Unplug your toaster when you aren't using it.
- Try to turn off the clock display on your oven, if possible. Even if you aren't cooking, that oven is still using juice to tell you the time.
- Don't open your oven to check on food. Every time you open the door to peep inside, you are releasing heat, which in turn means increasing the baking time. Which means upping your bill. If you have to peek, use the oven light to quickly check the progress, and make sure to turn it off when you finish.
- Group your kitchen counter appliances into one power strip, if possible. When you are not using them, flip the switch.
- Look for the ENERGY STAR logo whenever you buy new kitchen appliances. Those appliances have the government's approval for energy efficiency, which meets strict guidelines

of the U.S. Environmental Protection Agency as well as the
U.S. Department of Energy.

- Make sure to unplug any charger when the appliance (or
  cell phone) is completely charged.

We all may have our own opinions about going green or saving the planet. But, in this day and age, who doesn't want to save
a buck or two here and there? Besides, do you really want an electronic machine to get the best of you? Turn off those energy suckers so that you can overthrow the electronic mutiny that is being
waged right under your casserole-smelling nose.

Great Green Tip

Think plants are only for eating or enjoying? Think again! Not
only do plants offer the beauty of greenery in your kitchen, they
can also help you out in times of need! Keep an aloe plant on
hand to nurture any burns from your toaster or oven. Grow
lavender for its aromatic and relaxing fragrance. Create intoxicating tea from chamomile, and harvest the healing qualities of
echinacea. Your plant and herb friends are there for you in
times of need, so take the time to nurture and be there for
them.

Your Living Room: Live It

26. See the Light

Now that you have set up a functionally green kitchen, let's step into the living room. Wait! Before you leave your kitchen, take a moment to turn off the light. Flipping the switch is easy to forget, but it is also one of the easiest things to change. Before you leave any room, take the time to make sure you flip the switch and turn off the lights.

With little or no way to completely determine just how much electricity is wasted by leaving a light on, we are going to present a hypothetical example based on a formula from the Department of Energy–sponsored website, www.eere.energy.gov. The average cost for using an ordinary light bulb varies based on the type of bulb and fixture and a host of other variables.

Let's say you pay somewhere around 10 cents per kilowatt hour (kWh), and for 5 hours you leave on 5 different 50 watt light bulbs (5 x 50 w = 250 total watts); (250 watts x 5 hours) ÷ 1000 = 1.25 kWh x \$.10 = \$.125 x 30 days = \$3.75 per month. Based on these numbers, you are spending a little over 12 cents a day. Every day for a month, and you are up to \$3.75 for lights that you may not even be using. That may seem like chump change, but suppose that most of us leave those lights, and several more, on for far more than five hours. Imagine saving over \$45 a year just by flipping the switch for five lights. Small things do add up, and when you pair them with bigger lights you are talking about a multitude of savings in your electrical bill alone.

There are several ways to approach this problem:

- Simply flip the switch when you leave the room, as already mentioned.
- Use natural lighting. Open those blinds and let the sunshine do its thing!
- Try installing a dimmer in order to manually control the amount of light needed for a room. Doing so may seem expensive, but you will save money in the long run.
- Replace your regular light bulbs with energy-saving light bulbs.

Up to 75 percent less energy is used when lighting a room with energy-saving lightbulbs. And they do not give off as much heat as regular light bulbs. According to the U.S. Department of Energy, close to $8 billion a year in energy costs could be saved if every American home replaced just one of their bulbs with energy-saving light bulbs. If we all worked together to do this, greenhouse gases in the environment would be lowered by an equivalent of the emissions from close to 2 million cars. This goal is not only possible, but it only requires us to make a very simple change.

Here is where we enter a disputed area, though. The use of energy-saving bulbs is somewhat controversial based on the fact that they contain a small amount (less than what you would find in a watch battery) of mercury. To be overly cautious, these bulbs should not be thrown out with your regular trash. If the bulbs were to break and mercury leaked, prolonged exposure could lead to tremors, headaches, or nerve damage. (Mind you, there is more mercury in the watch battery that you may wear on your wrist every single day.) You can legally throw out these bulbs in most states, but since they are considered household hazardous waste, they should be taken to a designated disposal site or a center that recycles hazardous materials. If you already recycle, this is a small price to pay. The EPA recommends these websites when looking for a place to recycle your energy-saving bulbs: www.epa.gov/bulbrecycling and earth911.org.

What about a green solution to those back door or front door porch lights or your security lights? Here are some suggestions:

- Set your outside lights to turn on and off by a timer.
- Install a motion sensor to your outside lights if possible.
- Use energy-saving bulbs to cut down on cost and energy use if your outdoor porch lights take regular bulbs.
- Consider switching to solar-powered security lighting.

Which suggestion you choose is up to you. But, the important thing to remember is that a few small changes can make one large change in your electric bill—and make a difference in the world. Do the green, simple thing: flip the switch when you aren't using a light. Just that little effort will make a difference.

27. Squeeze the Tube

The day is over, dinner is digesting, the couch is calling, the dishwasher is washing, and that television clicker . . . was just around here somewhere. That's right. We are going to discuss your beloved television. Wait! Before you throw away our green book in a fit of rage, we watch television, too. Honestly, who doesn't?

On average, an American family watches over 8 hours of television every day. Ask yourself one question: How often is that television set on with no body in the reclining chair?

We aren't suggesting a ban on television. However, if you would like to save money on your electric bill, why not consider turning off the television? Here are a few simple suggestions to get you started:

- Turn it off. Step away from reality television for a night and turn on your own reality instead.
- Read a book.
- Reduce the number of televisions in your house to reduce your electric bill. If you have more than one television, make an effort to ensure that only one television is being watched at a time. Yes, this may require compromising with children and adolescents, or working out conflicting tastes. But, at least you will be watching together rather than in separate rooms.
- Try conversation with your family instead. Go ahead and have that lingering discussion about greenhouse gases and toxins. We know you want to!
- Make sure to watch with your kids if they are watching TV. Discuss what is on and try to start a dialogue with them about what they are watching. More often than not, they will become more interested in you and less interested in the screen.
- Make must-see television a couple or family event. This will greatly reduce the need for two televisions. If your tastes are very different, take turns each week. If you are single, make the decision to turn it off when you lose interest.

Your television, stereo, and DVD player are ghost devices that leach electricity even when they are turned off. Remember that digital clocks or displays still need juice to work. Plug all entertainment equipment into one power strip and flip the switch when you aren't watching.

Television can be a fun escape, but it doesn't have to be a nightly activity. The more you tune out the television, the more time you have for family, reading, yourself, and your friends. And you will be saving money, too!

Great Green Tip

Do you love curling up under the covers with a good book? Do you find it hard to pass a bookstore without buying your weight in books? If you are a book lover and you just can't get enough titles under your belt, try arranging a book exchange with your friends. Create your own library amongst your friends and circulate and reshelve.

28. Outside In

We all love nice things in our homes. Being surrounded by pretty things or knickknacks from our travels has a way of conjuring happy memories or bringing a sense of comfort and personality to our homes. Who doesn't enjoy a house full of personal touches and familial appeal?

One of the biggest traps in decorating is spending money on things to make our homes appear more welcoming or seasonal. Why spend money on decorations that attempt to create a natural or seasonal appeal when you can just step outside and bring nature into your home? Sure, it sounds a bit earthy and bohemian, but there are ways to create a chic and enviable look using what Mother Nature provides:

- Grow your own flowers and display them throughout your house. Flowers are beautiful, timeless, and classic.
- Harvest your own fruits and vegetables and display them in a glass vase. This is a lovely centerpiece for your table. Throw in walnuts, jewels, or unusual rocks to liven it up.
- Plant pumpkins or gourds to use as decorations in your house during the fall.
- Start your own small Christmas tree farm and harvest, and replant, your very own tree.
- Use pinecones to add spice and variety to floral arrangements. Or display the pinecones in a basket in your foyer.
- Bring fall foliage from your backyard to your living room. Display a few colorful leaves on your coffee table next to a few scattered books.
- Use tree stumps to create natural and earthy stools. Tie fabric around the top and change the colors of the fabrics for different seasons. If you have a fireplace, place your stool next to it for a natural, cozy nook.
- Use sand and seashells as colorful accents to your bathroom or for colorful arrangements in a vase.
- Collect unusual and shiny rocks and display them in vases, or use them in your office for paperweights. Or, use them to hold your bills together until you get around to paying them.

There are countless ways to bring chic and nature together. You don't have to buy the most expensive knickknacks to finish your home. You don't have to buy them at all. Step outside, harvest what nature provides, and create a warm, seasonal, and local environment in your own home. What better way to show the pride and excitement you have for where you live than to decorate from your own backyard?

29. Seek the Trashed Treasure

When it comes to furnishing your living room, buying just a couch, relaxing chair, or coffee table can often leave you scrounging for spare change or worried that you may need to take out a second mortgage on the house! Rather than buy new, try greener buying, or try finding green treasures for your home. The easiest way to redecorate your living room, for a fraction of the cost, is to become an artful scavenger. Why buy a new couch when used ones are at every corner? Why buy a new entertainment center when your neighbor is looking for a new home for his? Remember, there is no need to buy more when enough is already at your fingertips. Take a second look at secondhand items, and keep a sharp eye out for trashed treasures. You may find that the easiest way to decorate is the greenest way. Here are a few ways to seek greener living room treasures without cleaning out your pockets:

1. *Patrol your neighborhood.* Yard sales and moving sales are the greatest inventions ever. They are phenomenal places to find unique pieces for your home, like glorious retro chairs, fantastic end tables, and even unusual lamps. Just because other people are finished with their furniture doesn't mean that wonderful coffee table is ready to call it quits. It may need a little TLC, but for the price, you can roll up your sleeves and put a little refinishing time into your rare find.

2. *Get thrifty.* Thrift stores are one of the unsung heroes of used furniture. This may seem a bit too frugal for some, but don't knock it till you try it. Thrift stores are full of hidden treasures, and if you are persistent, your patience will be rewarded. You can find everything from lamps to telephones to used computers. Thrift stores are fantastic for finding all kinds of

furnishings, and you can artfully and tactfully piece together your entire living room for the price of one brand new end table.

3. *Take a second for secondhand.* Everybody knows somebody that knows somebody else with a couch or a computer desk that needs to be unloaded. It is so easy to get your hands on hand-me-down furniture—all you have to do is put the word out. There are stores that specialize in secondhand furnishings as well as antiques. Check out your local yellow pages to find them. You can also search the classified ads in your local paper or on Craigslist.org for things that are either gently used or unable to make a cross-country move. Paint it. Polish it. Leave it as is. Do whatever you like, just give it a second chance.

4. *Get inventive.* Before you decide to trash your old living room furniture, stop and take the time to search for a new way to bring it back to life. If you have a lamp that will no longer light your way, then try taking out the electrical wiring and light bulb base in order to create a decorative vase. Or, if your coffee table has seen one too many lattes, then consider putting it between your patio chairs for an outdoor coffee table, or in your garden as part of a meditation nook. You can paint it, sand it, or do whatever you like in order to make it fit more beautifully in another room or outside your home. If your coffee table has drawers, consider using it as a gardening storage table for your gardening needs. Before you decide to trash something, try to find a new use for it. Or, if you just have to bid it farewell, consider passing it to a neighbor. Give it away, or have a yard sale of your own. Making the choice to pass along useable furniture is the best way to ensure that the green buck doesn't stop with you.

5. *Go Dumpster diving.* Before you are disgusted by this option,

understand that we are not suggesting that you bury your-self in rotten lettuce to find a moldy piece of furniture. Far from it. What we are suggesting is that you check your local department stores, bookstores, toy stores, and nationwide chains for discontinued furniture, display furniture, or "damaged" furniture that has made its way from the showroom floor to the Dumpster. You would be amazed with what you can find. Think about it. How many times have you seen a display item that was chipped or slightly mistreated by hands-on shoppers? Where do you think those display items go? The green answer: they could go in your living room!

The important thing to remember is that throwing out functional furniture or always buying new doesn't have to be your first option. You can find ways to reuse furniture that is headed toward the Dumpster, or you can always pass along your old couch for the gently-used couch from your neighbor. If you do take the time to search for hidden treasures, then the tendency to discard rather than reuse may become a hand-me-down urban legend for the next generation.

Great Green Tip

Waging battle with those pesky energy ghosts? Don't forget about your computer! Remember to turn off your computer and monitor when you aren't using them, and make sure to plug your computer and printer into a power strip. If you haven't used the computer for more than twenty minutes, shut it down and flip the switch. Doing so will make sure that the computer doesn't use energy while no body sits before it. If you find yourself in the market for a new computer, make sure to check out the energy statistics. Knowing what to expect before you plug it in will ensure that you are getting the most energy-efficient use out of your computer.

30. Take a Load Off

So you have found your living room furniture by searching yard sales, participating in artful Dumpster diving, and by bringing nature inside to create a more rustic atmosphere. You're finished with greening your living room, right? Not exactly. Along with searching for green furniture options and using nature for your decorating needs, there is also a way to creatively prop your feet after a long day at work. Interested in finding a new way to use and recycle that magazine pile? Of course, you can choose to send those magazines to the recycling center, but why not spice up your living room with your own green, unique, handcrafted magazine stool? Here's what you need:

Old magazines
Twine or hemp thread
Basting brush
Glue
Piece of fabric (optional)
Lace, ribbon, or cording

1. Stack the magazines as tall as you would like your stool to be. If you prefer a stool with clean lines, use magazines of the same size. For an edgier look, try magazines of differing sizes. No matter which you choose, make sure to keep your stack manageable and tight.

2. Tie the magazines with twine or hemp thread. Run the twine under the magazines, and tie them lengthwise together on top. You may want to do this twice around, making parallel lines with your twine. Then tie it widthwise as well. Make sure to tie it as tightly as possible. The more times you tie it together, the better your stool will work.

3. To keep the edges of the magazines from fraying and tearing, use the basting brush to coat the sides with glue. Paint as many coats as desired.

4. You may want to decorate your stool with fabric. Cut and drape the fabric over the top of the stool and tie it with twine to secure it. You can use lace edging, ribbon, or cording to add flare. Simply glue the lace or ribbon onto the bottom of the fabric to create a finished look.

The best part of making your own stool is the personality that it will give your home. And you will have found a creative and green way to ensure that your beloved magazines can still be a part of your life. Although you can make alternative green choices for magazines, this way you will be using them, functionally, again, rather than sending them off after only one use.

Finding new and useful ways to reuse what you already have is the greenest and simplest way to make a difference. But the most important aspect of your magazine stool is that you are choosing to make a green statement. The next time you entertain guests, you can be sure that your unique creation will be a conversation piece for your green choices, allowing you to pass along green tips and potentially open a discussion about recycling and energy reduction. And you can bet on passing along your tip for making a personalized, recycled, and fully functional stool.

31. Light Your Green Fire

When the weather outside is frightful, the fireplace is so tempting and delightful. Some of the classic images of winter involve hot chocolate, crackling logs, cozy rugs, and snuggling next to the dancing flames in the fireplace. With all the heat that flows from the flames, a fireplace seems ideal for going green. It is natural, inviting, and one of the oldest forms of heat. So fireplaces should be used as an alternative heating source to counterbalance that skyrocketing heating bill, right? Wrong.

According to the U.S. Department of Energy, a traditional fireplace with a roaring fire can blow as much as 24,000 cubic feet of air per hour straight outside your home. This means that the warm air in your house will travel out of the chimney, and be replaced by cold air. Which then leaves your heat kicking on to regulate your house temperature, and working overtime, causing you to run in circles while trying to heat your home. Of course, the lure of a fireplace often outweighs the heat loss, so there are ways that you can still sip cocoa by the fire without sending your heat and your heating bill through the roof:

- Install glass doors on your fireplace to keep hot air from escaping. These doors come in handy when the fire is about to die but you can't close the flue due to the smoke.
- Turn down the heat, when you start a fire, to make sure that your thermostat doesn't work overtime to compensate for the air lost through the chimney.
- Make sure to close the flue when there is no fire since flues are designed to allow air to escape.
- Make sure to burn wood that is dry. Burning wet wood

causes excess smoke, and it will not burn as efficiently as dry wood.

- Turn on a ceiling fan to help circulate the heat coming from the flames. Hot air rises, and using your fan to push that air back down will help with using the heat to the fullest potential.
- If you enjoy the ambiance, try lighting a few candles in the hearth if building a fire is too much hassle. This will give you the illusion of the fire without the heat loss.

There is no disputing that the romantic allure of the fireplace is tempting and comforting. You don't have to stop using your fireplace if you have one. Understanding how they work in terms of heat loss and energy use will help alleviate many of the problems associated with fireplaces. Just thinking about the best times to light that fire, and possibly treating it as a special occasion for the family after a long morning of playing in the snow, will greatly reduce energy loss. Don't worry, you can still have your cocoa and drink it, too.

Great Green Tips

We all have that closet full of wrapping paper, falling out every time we open it and hitting us in the head while we search for that one elusive roll of paper that was "just in here, I know it." Before you head out to the store to buy a new roll of wrapping paper, try using old newspapers or magazines first. Or, give gift options that require no paper: gardens in a box, gifts in a jar, gift certificates, or trees. According to the Medical University of South Carolina's Office of Recycling and Solid Waste Management, if every American family chose to alternatively wrap 3 gifts during the holidays, they could save enough wrapping paper to cover 45,000 football fields! That is astounding. And with that amazing statistic, this section is all wrapped up.

Are you so busy working and greening your life that you rarely have time for friends? Do you worry that your friendships may just be falling by the wayside because of your lifestyle? Worry not, green friends. There are green ways to ensure that you are getting quality time, while still making a green contribution. The next time you run to the grocery, pick up a friend and double it! Not only will you be decreasing the amount of cars on the road, but she will also be able to do her weekly shopping right beside you, chatting and catching up on your life. Don't stop there, though! Take her along any time she may need to run an errand close to where you are headed. Take two friends when you can! The more the merrier, and you will be so content to have some friend time that you won't notice that you are performing double green duty: carpooling and decreasing air pollution!

Your Bedroom: Green Dreams

32. Between the Sheets

Now that you have turned off and unplugged your television and your computer, and you have made sure that each light is turned off when you leave your living room, let's journey into the sanctuary of the house: your bedroom. This is where you lay your head to sleep and where you expect to be able to release the pressures of the day and just relax. You don't sleep with a light on and you don't have trash to recycle in here, so how could this room need any greening? Go ahead and settle in for the night, snuggle under the covers, and read on.

One of the biggest compromises in any bedroom occurs between the sheets. Quilt or no quilt? Turn up the heat, or turn it down? And what two people can ever agree? It is guaranteed: if one person is freezing, the other is sweating buckets. So, to stop erupting into a fist fight during the pillow talk, here are a few green and simple ways to compromise under the sheets:

- Dress for the occasion. If you have a tendency to get cold while sleeping, then wear heavier pajamas. And vice versa when it comes to getting too hot. If you dress to suit your individual needs, your dreams will be cozy and you won't upset your bed companion.

- During the summer, use lighter sheets. Thinner sheets obviously do not weigh on you and will keep you cooler. Or, sleep without the sheets. Or, sleeping in the buff is always an option.
- Cover up during the winter. Use heavy sheets and make sure to add extra blankets. Throw a quilt between the sheets and the comforter to add a little extra warmth.
- If you are in need of new sheets, go extra green and buy organic. Doing so will ensure that you are avoiding any allergy-causing synthetic fibers or dyes.
- If your feet always get colder than the rest of your body, invest in a pair of thick, cozy socks to sleep in.
- If you have a ceiling fan, try turning it on just before you go to bed. If you are hot, a fan will circulate air enough to cool you before you turn in for the night. It can also circulate hot air in the winter. You may find that once you get your body regulated, you can turn it off for the night. But, if you need that slight bit of moving air, keep it on.

Regardless of whether you have a tendency to heat up or cool off during the night, it is important to remember that running to your thermostat should be the last resort. There are simple and effective ways to maintain or release the heat without ever having to leave the bed. And, you won't find yourself having constant arguments with your bedmate over the perfect temperature between the sheets.

33. Don't Let the Energy Bugs Bite

Staying comfortable in your bedroom is definitely necessary. However, according to the U.S. Department of Energy website, heating and cooling, through various systems in an average home, are responsible for 56 percent of your energy usage. In most cases, heating and cooling are the largest energy expenses in the home. Since we all want to be comfortable when we sleep, here are a few simple ways to lower that energy use and still snooze to your heart's delight:

- Open the windows in your bedroom when possible. This is the easiest way to cool a room. If the weather permits, allow the wind, sun, rain, and snow to do their thing.

- Use ceiling fans to circulate the air from your air conditioner to cool yourself. Even a stifling breeze will help to regulate your body temperature. Fans shouldn't be counted on to cool your entire home. But if you have a big enough ceiling fan in each room, you may not even have to turn on your air conditioner to find relief from the heat.

- Make sure that all vents and registers are clear and free to heat or cool the room as needed. If the register is covered, then you are blocking out the circulation of air. Before you decide to turn the thermostat up or down, double check your registers.

- Close the registers in any room you aren't using. It costs more in money and in energy to heat and cool every room in your home. When you leave the registers open in a room that you rarely enter, you are paying to heat or cool a room that nobody uses.

- Check your bedroom for leaks. Caulk any leaks that you may find in your insulation or windows.
- Use energy-efficient lights beside your bed for nighttime reading.
- In the winter, set your thermostat to 68°F during the day and lower at night; according to the U.S. Department of Energy, you can easily save energy and money this way. It may seem that you should have it warmer when you sleep, but if you have already added extra sheets, blankets, or jammies, then you are taking care of yourself rather than paying an energy company to do it for you.
- Set your thermostat to 78°F in the summer, only when you need cooling. Before you leave the house, make sure to set it for a higher temperature to avoid cooling an empty house. And vice versa for heating.
- Add plastic film to any single-paned windows in the winter to prevent cold air from coming in. Just be sure to seal the plastic tightly around the frame. If you live in an area that has extremely cold winters, try replacing your windows with double-paned windows. It may seem like an expensive alternative, but think about the money you will save on your energy bill in the long run.
- Use heavy curtains or draperies on your windows. In the winter the cold air can't pass through as easily. In the summer, they will block the sun and keep the room cooler.

We all want to be as snug as a bug when we sleep. However, using your thermostat to do what you can accomplish on your own with a few simple changes, allows money and energy to fly out the window. Take the time to consider how you want to conserve your energy in the bedroom. This is your place of sanctuary and rest. You don't want to drift off into dreamland only to have haunting images of that scary energy bill keeping you awake and restless. With these few simple changes, you can sleep peacefully, comfortably, and affordably.

Great Green Tip

Need a loud and obnoxious alarm clock to rouse you in the morning? Don't waste money and energy on large displays, clock radios, snooze buttons, timers, and digital thermometers. Use a wind-up alarm clock. When that alarm goes off at six in the morning, you will jump out of bed to shut it off. And you will be wide awake and ready to face the world rather than pushing the snooze button until you are late, scrambling for breakfast, and rushing out the door for work.

34. Get Picky

One of the most-used areas in your bedroom is your cluttered closet. Who hasn't bought a pair of pants on the run, only to find that they just aren't all they were cracked up to be? Or that pair of pants you keep just in case you lose a few more pounds or find the perfect place to wear them. We are all guilty of keeping unused clothing longer than we should. But now you don't have to feel guilty when you push them aside for the hundredth time. Pull them out, look them straight in the seams, and see the green.

Take Inventory

Go through your entire closet. Purses, shoes, ties, suits, pants, coats, hats, gloves. Look through it all and decide what you really want and what you really need.

The best rule of thumb when you check out a piece of clothing is to decide if you love yourself in it. If you are constantly tugging at it, trying to pull it down, unbuttoning it for more room, or trying to find something to match it, then you need to take it away from your closet. Remove it. Banish it. Put in your closet only what you will definitely wear on a regular basis. Keep special occasion clothes that truly fit and make you feel fabulous. Everything else needs to step aside. Now that you have a closet full of wearable and fabulous clothes, look through what is left behind and decide where it all should go. Here is where the fun part begins.

Have a Yard Sale

Sure, you aren't getting the exact money out of it that you put into it, but you are allowing another person to walk away with it and feel fabulous in it. And you aren't holding onto clothes for no reason while others can use them. Just don't use that yard sale money to go buy more clothes that don't fit!

Donate to Charity

There are many people out there who would truly love and wear the clothes that you don't wear any longer. Don't toss your clothing in the trash when you can donate them to a homeless shelter that can use them or a thrift store that can sell them for affordable prices. Your old winter coat could provide warmth for some shivering person searching for a light at the end of the tunnel. Be that light.

Set Up a Clothing Exchange with Your Friends

Invite your friends to come over with all of their unwanted clothes, shoes, purses, hats, gloves, and coats. You can have your own personal boutique while sharing the stories of your wrong purchases with each other. Trade purses. Share pants. Swap ties. Do whatever you like as long as you find a way to use your clothes rather than allow them to hang needlessly in your closet.

When you fall victim to buying those perfect purple shoes or that orange shirt that goes with absolutely nothing in your wardrobe, don't allow them to get the best of you. By donating or selling your clothing to someone who can use it, not only are you making sure that you are not wasting, but you are also recycling and reusing clothing that would otherwise waste away in your closet. There is no need for a friend or neighbor to waste gas, money, resources, and energy to buy another coat that has to be produced, shipped, taxed, and sold, when you have one that he or she could wear. Create the perfect streamlined wardrobe by making sure everything in your closest brings a smile to your face. Then you are getting the absolute best possible use out of your clothing—and your closet space!

35. Take the Time to Smell the Houseplants

Now that you have heavier curtains, cleared registers, extra blankets, perfect jammies, and toasty feet, it is time to settle in for a long sleep. You snuggle under the covers, adjust your body to that oh-so-perfect position, and then release one long, peaceful sigh. But, before you start snoring, how pure is that air you are inhaling? The average person spends one third of his or her life asleep. That would be, on average, 56 hours a week, 240 hours a month, and 2,920 hours a year. For a 74-year-old, that would be roughly 216,080 hours spent asleep! Since you spend one third of your life snoozing and deep-breathing, the air surrounding you should probably be as clean as possible.

One of the healthiest and easiest ways to green your air is to add more greenery. Indoor plants are excellent for producing oxygen as well as absorbing contaminants in the air. In fact, they are so good that NASA intends to use them in orbiting space stations! According to the EPA, some of the air pollutants within your home may include: asbestos from insulation, combustion sources such as coal or wood, wet carpeting, and chemicals from household cleaning products. Even the pressed wood furniture used in nightstands can cause air pollution within your home.

According to the Clean Air Gardening website, there are several houseplants available at your local nursery that are excellent in helping clear the air:

- Peace lily
- English ivy
- Spider plant
- Bamboo or reed palm
- Chinese evergreen
- Weeping fig

These are only a few of the options available. The basic idea is that the more greenery you add to your home, the greener your air will become. Every time you release carbon dioxide in to the air, those plants will inhale it, convert it, and breathe out sweet oxygen for your lungs. Yes, your plants do love you just that much!

Although adding plants to your bedroom is the least expensive way to green your air, there are other options as well. So, if you just really don't trust your green thumb:

- Use an air filtration system. This option is definitely more expensive, but the air filters within them are certain to clear the air.

- Make sure to keep your pillow clean and free of dust mites and other allergens. Clean your pillow or vacuum it when you change your sheets.

- When it is time to buy another pillow, choose one that is made of organic, all natural materials such as cotton, natural latex, or buckwheat rather than synthetic fibers or dyes.

- Vacuum your mattress when you change your sheets. This removes allergens and dust mites that may be keeping you from getting a good night's sleep.

- Try using all natural polishes when you can. Aerosol furniture polish chemicals and fumes can be hard on your lungs and throat. If you can't find all natural polishes in your store, use a mixture of vinegar and olive oil to polish your furniture.

Before it is time to turn in for the night, make sure that your bedroom environment is green and clear of unwanted allergens, perfumes, and other toxins. Take the time to add a few plants to your bedroom, and then take a deep breath. Do you feel it? Smell it? That is fresh, green, and clean natural air. Just the way Mother Nature intended.

Great Green Tips

Tired of stinky moth balls in your closet? Try creating a natural moth deterrent as well as an aromatic freshener for your closet. All you need are some whole cloves and an orange. Punch the cloves into the orange making sure to completely cover it with cloves. Twist a screw into the top of the orange and tie a string or a ribbon to hang it in the closet. Not only will your clothes smell tangy, but the winged eaters will be wary of attacking your linens and other things. It will stay fragrant long after the orange dries. Give yourself a delightful boost in your own closet, or give them away as fantastic housewarming gifts.

Is your hair driving you crazy? Have you spent months growing it out, only to wish that you never had to see another conditioner, hair dryer, or flat iron? Before you rush off to the salon to whack that unmanageable hair, take the time to make a decision that may change the life of a child. Consider donating your hair to Locks of Love. Locks of Love is a nonprofit organization that is dedicated to providing hairpieces to needy children suffering from hair loss due to medical reasons. You could make a significant difference in a child's life, and you will be finding a new way to reuse what is no longer useful to you. Go to www.locksoflove.org to check out how to correctly cut your hair in order to donate. Before you chop it, make the decision to reuse it. Somewhere, a child in need will thank you.

Your Bathroom: Lather, Rinse, Reuse

36. Put On Your Green Shower Cap

Now that your bedroom is plant friendly, naturally lit, and affordably green, let's move on to another sanctuary of your home: your bathroom. With baths to be taken, teeth to be brushed, toilets to be . . . ahem . . . used, the main green issue lurking in your bathroom has to deal with water consumption.

Conserving water in the bathroom once again brings up the bath vs. shower debate. For most of us, slipping into a hot bath is the perfect way to relax and unwind. But, when you take the time to compare the water consumption numbers, you may find that taking a bath often leaves your money flowing right down the drain.

According to the Consumer Energy Center website, an average bath uses anywhere from 30 to 50 gallons of water. That may not seem like a lot until you compare it to the 20 gallons of water used in a four-minute shower. Think about the fact that a bath could potentially be using 30 more gallons of water. Water that you will ultimately send straight down the drain. Which is better, shower or bath? The answer may not be so obvious. It all depends on factors like person, showerhead, or bathtub size.

The easiest way to determine how much water you use when showering is to simply plug the drain the next time you take a shower.

See how much water is left standing in the tub when you are finished. If it is less than you would use to take a bath, then a shower may be the water-saving route for you. If you have a wading pool around your calves, then you may actually be using about the same amount or less for a bath. Each faucet, person, and drain can vary, so the best option is the option that best fits you.

There are other ways to conserve water and energy whether taking a bath *or* a shower:

- *Scrub in the tub.* When you do decide to indulge in a bath, make sure to *wash* in the bath as well. Soaking in the tub and then showering to finish washing only wastes more water.

- *Drain train.* Make sure to close the drain before turning on the water to take a bath. Sure, it will be cold at first, but leaving it running until the water warms before you plug the drain only sends useful water straight down the drain. Once the water warms, it will heat that initial cold water.

- *Cool it.* Try not to take a scorching shower. Choosing to take a bit of a cooler shower will not only wake you, but it will also give your hot water heater a break. Taking a shower that is cooler will use less energy to heat the water, and in turn save you money.

- *Keep it short.* The next time you take a shower, pay attention to how long you need to wash and how long you just stand there, letting the water wash over you. That time spent under the water is soothing, but it is also wasteful and unnecessary. Try to shorten your shower time. If you reduce your time in the shower by just one minute, you could save 1,825 gallons of water per year. Think about all those gallons of water you will be saving. If you want those extra green points, try to keep your showers somewhere around four to five minutes. This may not seem like much time, but once you begin to shorten your time under the water, you may find that taking a four-minute shower isn't as hard to do as you thought.

- *Multitask.* Try brushing your teeth in the shower. Since you already have it on, why not use that water to clean your teeth as well. While you wait for that conditioner to set, give your mouth a bit of conditioning as well. If you want extra green points, try multitasking and brushing with baking soda.

- *Double it.* If you have small children, and you are comfortable with it, put them in the tub or shower together. This will give them a playmate, and you may find that you also have a moment of peace while they splash and take turns pouring water over each other's heads.

- *Use your head.* One of the easiest ways to conserve water and your money is to install a low-flow showerhead. You could reduce your shower from 20 gallons to 10 gallons in the time it takes to screw on a showerhead. This is an inexpensive improvement to your shower that could save you gallons of water after only one use.

- *Go overboard.* If you really want to focus on saving energy and water, you can try turning off the water while you scrub. This is commonly called a "navy shower," but campers should be familiar with this as well. Turn the water on to rinse. Then turn it off while you lather up. Turn it back on only to rinse again. This may seem extreme, but considering the amount of water and money you can save, you may just want to go overboard and go navy.

These are only a few ways to get started with saving energy and water. Does this mean that you have to forsake long, luxurious baths for quick showers in which you race to shave, brush your teeth, shampoo, rinse, and condition all in under five minutes? Of course not. You can still take baths. Just make them a treat for yourself. And, make sure to take smarter baths rather than hotter baths. Your water bill will thank you.

37. Unflush Your Money Down the Drain

There is one fixture in your bathroom that gets more use than any other: your toilet. We aren't going to go into the logistics of toilet use, nor are we going to discuss where the waste being flushed down a toilet ultimately ends up. What we do need to discuss, however, are the little-known facts about the average family's toilet use.

According to the EPA, an average family of four goes through 400 gallons of water a day. Nearly 30 percent of that water use comes from flushing the toilet—that's about 120 gallons a day, or roughly 30 gallons per person. An average person will flush the toilet around 140,000 times in a lifetime. Let's reduce that average number to three people per household. With 3.5–5 gallons of water used with every flush in traditional toilets, that averages out to about 490,000–700,000 flushed gallons of water per person or 1,470,000–2,100,000 gallons of water per household in a lifetime.

Although these numbers are alarming, we can't simply refuse to use indoor plumbing because of the water waste involved. So, unless you want to return to the days of the outhouse, you have little choice, right? Well, sort of. There are simple ways to reduce the amount of water used by you and your toilet.

Be a Mellow Fellow

The first obvious difference you can make is simply to choose not to flush every time. If it's yellow, let it mellow. If it's brown, flush it down. However, leaving a little mellow yellow in the toilet could prove a bit embarrassing when you entertain, so make the choice to do it when you can, and if it suits you.

Be a Jug Head

Remember that half-gallon milk jug we discussed before? Well, here is your chance to use it in yet another way. When you finish your milk, rinse out the half-gallon jug and fill it full of sand or rocks. Place it in the tank of your toilet and flush as usual. The filled jug will displace the water, using a half-gallon less water with each flush. Just make sure that the jug clears all working parts of your toilet. If it should fall over, it could cause your toilet to run continuously in a vain attempt to refill.

Go Low

With a water-efficient, low-flow toilet, that is. If you are in the market for a new toilet, talk to a salesperson, or go online and check out the EPA-sponsored program called WaterSense. This program is designed to help consumers when purchasing a new water-efficient toilet. There are toilets on the market that can greatly reduce the amount of water used, but still pack the mighty flush that we all count on. In fact, these toilets are efficient enough to reduce that number of 3.5–5 gallons a flush to 1.3 gallons a flush. That is a significant difference. According to the EPA, installing a low-flow toilet could save you 4,000 gallons of water a year, and if every home in the United States used a low-flush toilet, we could save 640 billion gallons of water a year. That is more water than what flows over Niagara Falls in two weeks' time.

We all have to use it. There is no way around flushing your toilet, but you can make small affordable adjustments, or just use conservational sense. Don't flush water or your money down the toilet unless it is truly necessary.

Great Green Tip

Do you feel guilty about that excess water running down the drain while you wait for warm water to wash or shave your face? Feel guilty no more. Put a half-gallon milk jug next to or under your sink, and when it comes time to let your water warm for a daily scrub or shave, collect the excess cold water in the jug. Use it to water your plants or however you like, just make sure to let your guilt go down your drain, not your water.

38. The Tooth of It All

Whether you do it once a day, twice a day, or once a week, your momma always told you (and your dentist may have scolded you) to make sure you brush your teeth. Taking care of our teeth has become a national obsession, with choices about which kind of electric toothbrush to buy or which bleach will whiten your teeth to glow-in-the-dark bright. What often escapes our attention, however, is the amount of water wasted while brushing, flossing, and humming your way through the prescribed two minutes of oral hygiene twice a day.

Two minutes may seem like a small amount of time to worry

about water use. After all, we have already described the money-saving tip of four-minute showers. But consider this: your two minutes of brushing, if the water is left running, could account for up to 14 gallons of wasted water in older faucets (according to the EPA). Water faucets are responsible for 15 percent of the average household's indoor water use. That percentage adds up to more than one trillion gallons of water a year in the United States. That is an amazing amount of water that could be going down the drain while you brush your two minutes away, and listen to the sound of your running faucet.

There are several ways to make your brushing experience greener:

1. *Turn it off.* According to the EPA, you can save up to 3,000 gallons of water a year by simply turning off the water while you brush your teeth. Wet it. Turn it off. Paste it. Brush. Rinse. By using as little water as possible to brush your teeth, you are making a real difference not only in the amount of water available in the United States, but also in your water bill.
2. *Multitask.* As mentioned before, brush while you are in the shower. Or you can use the water you collect while waiting for your tap water to warm to wash your face. Any time you have excess water or you are performing a task with water, wet your brush and do your thing! Every little bit helps.
3. *Accessorize.* According to the EPA, just by adding faucet accessories such as water-saving aerators, you can reduce water use by approximately 30 percent. Aerators are designed to mix air with water, allowing for a smooth flow. Water-saving aerators will still provide that smooth flow while using less water.
4. *Use your sense.* While modern faucets do not exceed 2.2 gallons of water per minute, older faucets often allow for 3–7 gallons per minute. You can reduce this number by going with a WaterSense faucet. WaterSense (a partnership program

sponsored by the EPA) faucets reduce the amount of water flow to 1.5 gallons per minute. Just by installing one, you could save more than 500 gallons of water a year. If you prefer to hold on to your existing faucet, simply install a WaterSense aerator. Doing so could save water as well as decrease your energy bill by slowing your hot water heater use.

By simply installing an aerator or purchasing a WaterSense faucet, we could potentially save $600 million nationally in energy costs as well as 60 billion gallons of water a year. Imagine those billions of gallons of water going where they could be most needed: severely depleted areas within our own country suffering from the effects of drought. According to the EPA, 60 billion gallons of water is enough to meet the public demand for water in Miami for 150 days. Imagine the change you can bring about by simply turning off the faucet for two minutes while you brush!

39. Go Natural and Green Clean

When it comes to cleaning your house, the one area that seems to get the most attention, and the most disinfecting, is the bathroom. We have become so accustomed to using harsh chemicals, bleach, and strong-smelling toilet cleaners that we associate the smell of these items with a clean bathroom.

But how tried and true are these cleansers? Sure, they clean and disinfect your bathroom, but at what price? There was a time when people cleaned their homes without harsh manufactured chemicals—how did they function?

They used what has always worked: Simple, effective, everyday ingredients like soap and water, vinegar, salt, and baking soda. Okay, before you say these have no harmful effect on bacteria or mold (which can harm you), let's go back to Newton. For every action of eradicating and overly sterilizing our home, we are causing the reaction of disrupting the natural, effective, and delicately balanced world of bacteria. We're not saying that you should become fast friends with your toilet bacteria, but using abrasive and chemical-ridden cleaners to attack the bacteria may just be doing our bodies more harm than good. With *no* bacteria allowed anywhere in your home, you may be killing off helpful bacteria that often ward off harmful bacteria. There are ways to kill harmful bacteria, disinfect your toilet and bathtub, and clean your sinks without using stringent chemicals.

If you are concerned about the potential harm in those hard-to-pronounce ingredients on the back of your bathroom cleaner, but you'd like to avoid the guesswork involved with mixing your own cleaner, you can seek out commercial bathroom cleaners that offer safer ingredients. While many of these newer, green cleaners were once available only at natural food stores, they have made their way into the mainstream supermarket. Many of them use natural cleaning agents such as vinegar, lemon, ethanol-based alcohol, or natural oils. These products are very competitively priced, and they are often less expensive than the traditional, chemical-based cleaners. So the next time you are in the supermarket searching for an affordable, greener cleaner, opt for the eco-friendly option.

If you are a more adventurous do-it-yourself type, and you would like to avoid *buying* when you can create your own, you can easily make your own toilet or bathtub cleaner. There are several everyday cleaning ingredients lurking in your cabinets:

- *Baking soda.* Not only can this wonderful cleaning agent cleanse the odors from your fridge, but it is also amazing when it comes to scrubbing a tub. Sprinkle some baking soda into

the tub, wet it, and scrub with a sponge. It will make a paste
similar to that of commercial brand cleansers. When you have
worked it into a nice scrubbing lather, rinse it and watch as
your tub shines just as it would had you used harsh chemicals. You can also unclog bathroom drains with it. Once a
week, pour ¼ cup baking soda down your drain. Follow it
with boiling water to clean unwanted clogs. Repeat if necessary. You can also combine baking soda with water, vinegar,
salt, or lemon juice to use throughout your home.

- *White distilled vinegar.* This everyday household ingredient is
an excellent cleaner for mildew, dirt, and grease. Pair it with
baking soda, and you have a practical, all-purpose green cleaner.
To clean and deodorize your toilet, pour in baking soda, follow it with vinegar, allow the mixture to fizz and bubble,
and then scrub your toilet with a brush. This will leave your
bowl sparkling clean. To fight that soap buildup on your tub,
spray it with vinegar, allow it to set, and then follow through
with a baking soda scrub. Scrub your bathroom sinks in the
same manner. You can also try mixing vinegar with water to
create a natural and effective glass cleaner for your bathroom
mirrors. Vinegar is also an excellent way to fight lime deposits
and mildew. And, as we mentioned before, you can rid your
sink of pesky gnats by leaving out a capful of cider vinegar
mixed with a few drops of dishwashing liquid. They will be
drawn to it, and their greediness will be the death of them.

- *Hydrogen peroxide.* Try using it to remove mold and buildup
in your bathtub or shower. If you find stains to be a problem, or if your buildup is stubborn, spray straight hydrogen
peroxide onto the stain and allow it to penetrate before scrubbing. This is also useful for disinfecting and bleaching. For
more general cleaning, mix the peroxide in a 50/50 solution
with water.

- *Salt.* You can use salt as an abrasive scrubbing agent, or mix it with vinegar to clean copper or brass. You can also dip a lemon slice into salt to clean tarnished brass or copper or to fight rust. The lemon breaks it up, and the salt creates a mild abrasive cleaning agent.

- *Lemon juice.* Those chemical cleaners that add the artificial smell of lemons have the right idea, but the wrong approach. Even without the harsh chemicals, lemon juice is a powerful cleaning agent. Use it to mix with vinegar and/or baking soda to create a cleaning paste. Lemon juice is great for cutting through soap scum and dissolving hard water deposits. You can also use it to clean or shine brass or copper!

With the green cleaners that are popping up on store shelves, and the ingenuity of do-it-yourself cleaning, it is possible to create a clean, green, and chemical-free bathroom and home. If you do worry that green cleaners aren't as potent or effective as the chemical antibacterial variety, just remember that the best line of defense in fighting off unwanted bacteria doesn't always mean using chemicals that are harsh on your hands, lungs, and homes. Using soap and hot water is still the best way to fight off dirt, germs, and bacteria. And then use inexpensive, green, and completely effective cleaning ingredients to green clean your bathroom.

Great Green Tip

Tired of constantly collecting and washing towels after every shower? Try lightening your load by reusing your bath towels. You are clean when you get out of the shower, right? How dirty could that towel possibly be after one use? Allow your towel to dry on a rack and reuse it at least three times before

chucking it in the laundry. You will not only lighten your work-
load, but you will also save water, energy used to wash and
dry the towels, and, of course, your money!

40. Everything but the Bathroom Sink

With green-cleaned sinks and bathtubs, thrice-used towels,
four-minute showers, and water-saving teeth brushing now
becoming a part of your green household, it would seem impossible
to add any more green tips to the bathroom, right? Think again, green
friend. With so many ways to green your bathroom, and save a little extra money to boot, we decided to throw them all together.
Start with something easy:

- Set a romantic mood, and bathe by candlelight every once
  in a while.
- Recycle those shampoo, conditioner, hairspray, and body wash
  bottles.
- When you find a conditioner that didn't exactly meet your
  conditions, try using it for shaving gel rather than throwing
  it out. You will get two products for the price of one.
- Men: throw a fog-proof mirror on the shower wall, and shave
  while you bathe, condition, or rinse. Women: to save water,
  try turning off the water while you shave your legs.
- Check for and repair any leaky faucets. A little dribble can
  turn into several gallons without you knowing. Fix that little
  annoying drip that could potentially turn into a money drain.

Once you have mastered those subtle changes, try these:

- *Unplug all hair dryers, flat irons, curling irons, or other irons as soon as you are finished with them.* This goes for rechargeable razors as well as toothbrushes. Once they are charged, unplug them. Remember, electrical equipment can eat up electricity even when you aren't using them.
- *Weed out any and all styling products that haven't been used in the past six months.* If you aren't using them, give them away, or if they are nearly empty, use them and recycle the bottles. Buy less, use less, save more.
- *Turn on the water only to rinse your razor while shaving.* Allowing the water to run while shaving is wasteful. Filling the sink with hot water is a better option, but using a quick burst of water and then turning it off is the best way to avoid wasting water.
- *Let your hair dry naturally.* Sure, there are times when a hair dryer is more practical and necessary when it comes to styling wayward and unruly hair. However, there are times when you just aren't planning to go anywhere. So, rather than plug it in, unplug it, put it away, and let your hair dryer and your hair have a day off.

When you are ready for something a bit more challenging:

- *Switch from plastic shower curtains and liners to water-repellant cloth ones.* Rather than throwing them away when they become dirty, you can often throw them in the washer and re-hang them for many more showers to come. For extra green points, try an organic shower curtain.
- *Use nondisposable razors.* According to the educational, non-

profit organization, Eco-Action, about 2 billion disposable razors end up in landfills every year. Admittedly, they are extremely handy while traveling, but why buy something to use once and then throw it away if you can make the choice to get a reuseable one? Make the more expensive purchase of a nondisposable razor. In the long run, you will save money by reusing rather than just using and tossing. If you want to go the extra green mile, buy a rechargeable razor. You don't have to constantly change the blades, and you get the green satisfaction of knowing you aren't adding to a landfill. If you really want the top honors in the green classroom, search for recycled and recyclable razors.

- *Go natural.* Use creams, shampoos, beauty products, styling products, makeup, and lotions that are made from natural products as well as packaged in recycled and recyclable materials. Sure, this can be pricey, but if you feel the need to fully make over your bathroom supplies, there are options out there for greener products. Just make sure to check the label to ensure you are getting what you pay for. Don't always assume that corporations are doing their part to green the world, especially when there is money to be made just by putting "green" in the title.

Whew! With so many green possibilities hiding in your bathroom, it can be a bit overwhelming to tackle it all at once. So, don't. Do what feels natural, easy, and greenest for you. There are countless simple ways to save money, energy, and a little bit of the Earth if you only take the time to make little changes. Every small change leads to a bigger change, which will eventually lead to global change. So go ahead and get that ball rolling toward global change from your own green bathroom.

Your Laundry Room:
Green Money Laundering

41. Lighten Your Load

With a green-cleaned bathroom sparkling behind you, let's move to the other stain-fighting, germ-killing, towel-filled room in your home: the laundry room. Along with the fantastic invention of indoor plumbing came the marvels of the washing machine and dryer. The question is, are you getting all that you possibly can out of their services? Don't worry—we aren't pushing the return of a washboard, lye soap, and a babbling brook. Although, if you do feel the tug to go back to the very basics, we salute you and we won't discourage you!

The green approach to doing energy-efficient laundry falls into two categories: headwork energy, and machine energy. What we mean by headwork energy is that there are several ways to reduce your energy input and output before and during your everyday laundry chores. But you have to use some brain power along with a little bit of trial and error.

With over-the-top commercials for new and improved laundry detergents and fantastic chemical stain removers, along with hot water/ cold water detergent debates, it can be a little confusing and expensive to attempt a green change in the laundry room. However, there are a few simple tips to save time, water, and energy.

Divide and Conquer

Color, texture, and cycle coordinate. Not all clothes wash alike. Therefore, you have to approach your laundry selectively to get the most
from your clothes, your washer and dryer, and your money. Make
sure to separate lights from darks to avoid bleeding, towels from
clothes to avoid lint, and sturdy clothes from delicates to avoid tearing delicate clothes or under washing heavier clothes. Dividing your
laundry into heavy and light, and lights and darks, will not only
save time, but will also help in avoiding using excess water and drying time. Similar fabrics will wash and dry similarly.

Enough Is Enough

One of the most confusing things about using that little scoop inside the box of detergent is determining whether or not you are dealing with a small, medium, or large load. If you have a few towels
and socks together, would that be a large load due to the towels,
a small load due to the socks, or a medium load because you just
have no idea and opt for the in-between choice?

Most often, the in-between choice seems logical. However, the choice
between small, medium, and large actually depends on the water
level (your detergent and water have to work together adequately),
the spacing of the clothes within the washer, and whether or not
you have a front-loading washer or a conventional top-loading washer.
Confusing, right? Don't fret. Although laundry may seem overwhelming at times, what you need to concentrate on, for the most
part, is how much water you need to use for your laundry to move
freely, and then add detergent based on that amount of water. Adding
too much detergent will only cause detergent "clumping" on your
clothes; or you will succeed in sending more detergent down the
drain, and spending more money in the long run. Adding too little

may not get your clothes as clean as you would like. The best way to make sure you are getting the most out of your detergent without wasting is to simply look at your clothes load and your water level, and then take the time to read that measuring cup.

Cool It

Now that you have divided, sorted, scooped, and loaded, there is the question of washing cycles. Hot vs. cold. Permanent press vs. sturdy. And what exactly determines the regular/normal cycle? So many choices!

The first thing to consider is whether your dirty clothes need a firm hand, or a gentle touch, cool breezes, or desert climates, and firm or gentle spins. Since the most energy used during a washing cycle is for heating hot water, in order to make a greener choice, try to reserve that sturdy/hot water cycle for truly dirty or need-to-kill-bacteria loads. When you are doing an everyday load of regular clothes, try washing with cold water. Your clothes will get just as clean, and you can now buy cold water detergents that actually work with your cold water choices to adequately clean your clothes. You can also use traditional detergent with cold water, but most often, that detergent works best in hot water. Either way, try washing with cooler water whenever possible. And make sure to use the correct cycle to avoid overwashing your clothes and using unnecessary energy and water.

Dry Ideas

Before you move on to drying your clothes, make sure that most of the water has been removed or wrung out of your laundry. The less water you have dripping from your socks, sweaters, and pants, the less time and energy needed to dry them.

Whether you are a laundry novice or a pro, there are many things you can do to save energy in the laundry room. Before you decide to throw in that next load of laundry, take the time to sort, coordinate, and cycle plan. It may seem like a lot of work, but once you take the time to work out a system, you'll be a household laundry aficionado in no time!

42. Tumble Dry Lowdown

Now that you have mastered the headwork energy and created a productive, time and money–saving system, let's move on to machine energy. According to the Natural Resources Defense Council website, while most people assume the motor is the energy-sucking culprit in a washer, 90 percent of the energy used actually comes from heating the water. There are easy ways to avoid using excess energy when it comes to water use.

Be Water-Level-Headed

Use only the amount of water necessary for each individual load. Not only are you wasting water when allowing the washer to overfill, but you are also making your washing machine work harder when rinsing and spinning. Less water, less work for your machine. Making sure the water level is adequate for washing does not always mean allowing the water to rise above the clothes. Remember, the clothes, if not overloaded, will shift, twist, turn, and submerge during the wash cycle. You need to only observe a load or two to get the hang of how much water you really need. Watch the clothes and make sure that they are moving easily through the water. You need only enough water to allow free movement. If your clothes are so submerged you have to search for them, you are using too much water. Should your clothes be higher than the water, you are using too little. It takes a little trial and error and patience to get it right.

Chill Out

Use cold water when possible. Using hot water for every load causes your hot water heater to work overtime. Give your hot water heater a break and cool it down. With the cold water detergents that are available, you can get nearly all your clothes just as clean without all the steam.

Be Efficient

Don't dump your useful and fully functional washer for a new, energy-efficient one, but if you are shopping for a new washing machine anyway, consider buying the energy-efficient washers that are available. These are often front-loading washers and many of them use less water and energy. According to the U.S. Department of Energy, washers boasting the ENERGY STAR label can wash clothes using 50 percent less energy. These washers also use 18–25 gallons of water whereas standard washers can use up to 40 gallons per load. They also spin the clothes more efficiently, which allows for less drying time.

Let's move onto the washing machine's greatest companion: the dryer. Although you can't avoid using electricity when using a dryer, there are simple and energy-efficient ways to get the most out of your drying experience.

- *Dry full loads.* Remember, you are using the same amount of energy to dry a few items as you are to dry a large load.
- *Separate heavy loads from light loads.* Those socks may already be dry and merely taking up valuable dryer space while those heavy towels continue to flip, flop, and re-wet everything in the dryer.
- *Don't overdry.* If you don't have a dryer that detects when clothes are dry, then try actually checking them out yourself during the cycle. Once you have an idea whether or not your clothes need a full cycle, you will be better able to judge the time needed next time you dry a similar load.
- *Use the heat.* Ever noticed that your dryer stays hot for a while after you pull the warm, sweet-smelling clothes out? That is because of residual heat. Try throwing in another load of wet clothes just after removing dry ones. Taking advantage of that heat will dry clothes quicker and save energy.
- *Lose the lint.* Clean your lint filter after every load to make sure the air properly circulates and to avoid longer drying times. If you use fabric softener sheets, make sure to test to see if waxy buildup has accumulated on the lint filter. To check for buildup, run water over your lint filter; if the water does not easily flow through, try gently brushing it with a soft bristle brush to remove the buildup.

Washers and dryers were invented to save time. So why are we advising investing so much time in "helping" the washer and dryer do their jobs? Because in the long run, taking the time to accurately and efficiently wash and dry your clothes will not only put money back into your pocket, your clothes, and the longevity of your washer and dryer, but you also get the added boost of adding a few green points to your environmental credit card. Take the time to make the time for green laundering. The Earth and your clothes will thank you.

Great Green Tip

Tired of searching for that elusive match to your wayward socks? Don't despair, and don't get rid of that matchless mate. Instead, try giving that sock another life:

- Pull it over your hand and create an efficient and effective dusting glove.
- Fill it halfway with catnip, tie off the end, and give your kitty a much-deserved treat.
- Fill it with dry beans, sew the ends closed, and turn it into a beanbag for a beanbag toss during family fun day.
- Fill it with fish gravel, cut away the elastic, and sew the ends together to create a funky coaster, or use it as a trivet.
- Cut each sock into narrow strips, and weave them together for a fun, decorative potholder.
- Fill it with uncooked rice (not the minute variety), sew the open end together, throw it in the microwave for a few seconds, and use it for a portable, natural heating pad for aches and pains. (Add a little scented oil if you plan to give it for a gift!)

43. A Mixed Load of Laundry Tips

We have discussed detergent, water, and energy, so could there possibly be more tips for saving energy and money when it comes to doing laundry? Don't worry, we wouldn't leave you hanging out to dry without handing out a few more useful green tips to get you through your laundry and to add a few more pennies to your pocket. So, before we leave the suds and bubbles behind, check out these energy-saving bonus tips.

Wear Your Clothes More Than You Wash Them

With the convenience of a washer and a dryer, we often overlook the obvious question about our clothes: Are they really dirty? Sure, some things shouldn't be worn more than once, but some items may be worn again before being tossed into the laundry.

Read the Labels

One of the easiest ways to wash, clean, and shrink your new favorite shirt is to ignore the cleaning instructions. Make sure to follow the directions to avoid needlessly damaging your clothing and save time and energy in your wash cycle.

Avoid Dry-Cleaning When Possible

Dry-cleaning facilities use a chemical cleaning solvent called perchloroethylene, or "perc" for short. According to the EPA website, prolonged exposure to perc can result in dizziness, fatigue, nausea, and skin and lung irritation, to name a few. And, according to the Coalition for Clean Air website, 1 out of every 10 public drinking wells in California have been contaminated with perc. If it is happening in California, could it be happening in your neighborhood as well? If your clothes need special cleaning that you can't provide, consider a wet-cleaning facility. These cleaners use a system of water and non-toxic detergents to gently clean your delicate fabrics, whereas dry cleaners traditionally use chemicals to treat your clothes, never actually getting them "wet" in a washing machine.

Line Dry Your Clothes

When possible, line dry your clothes. In warm weather, take advantage of the sun power and fresh flowers and dry your clothing outside. Although the fresh smell may be incentive enough, think about the energy you will save by not using your dryer! In cooler weather, you can use a drying rack or line inside your house.

Avoid "Crunchy" Clothes

One of the drawbacks to line drying your clothing is "crunchy" clothes. To prevent this, add ¼–½ cup white vinegar to your rinse cycle in the washer. The vinegar will act as a natural fabric softener, leaving your clothes to dry softly on the line.

Get Hot and Steamy

When the time comes to attack the wrinkles inevitably created by the dryer, try hanging the clothes in the bathroom while you shower. The hot steam actually removes the wrinkles just as effectively as a hot iron, without using any additional energy.

Make a Patch Work

Skip the tailor and try mending your clothing yourself. Rather than tossing out clothes with a missing button or loose seam, try restitching, patching, and threading them. Learning how to repair your own clothes will not only increase their longevity, but you will also save money by fixing them yourself rather than taking them to a professional. Go ahead and give it a try! What have you got to lose?

Do-It-Yourself Detergent

If you are ready to ditch the store-bought detergent, try making and using your own! To make your own detergent you will need:

> *2 cups finely grated soap (you can use any kind of leftover*
> *bar soap)*
> *1 cup washing soda (you can find this in the laundry aisle*
> *at your local store)*
> *1 cup borax (usually found around the prewash/soaking agents)*

1. Mix all the ingredients together and store it in an air-tight container.
2. Use 2 tablespoons per load of dirty clothes, and wash as usual!

Really, that's it! It is just that simple. And cost efficient. For what you spend on commercial laundry detergents, you could wash hundreds of loads with your own, homemade, powerful detergent.

Stain Solutions

To do more than just make your own detergent, check out these fierce natural stain fighters:

- *Liquid soap.* Liquid dishwashing soap (or even hand soap) is one of the best stain fighters out there. Just dab—don't rub—the wet stain with cold water (warm or hot water can set the stain), put some liquid soap on it, add a bit of water, and scrub. An old toothbrush makes a great scrubbing tool. Once you have effectively treated your stain, launder as usual.
- *Hairspray.* To treat an ink stain, try spraying hairspray on it. The alcohol in the hairspray usually works miracles on ink.

Just make sure to put a paper towel or an old rag under the stain to catch the excess ink when it runs off. If you don't have hairspray, try using rubbing alcohol.

- *Your freezer.* For gum, candle wax, or melted crayon stains, try putting your clothes in a plastic bag and freezing them. Once the gum or wax gets cold enough, you should be able to scrape it from the garment with a butter knife or a credit card.

- *Milk.* There is nothing worse than a wine stain on a new white shirt. Most often, you can dab and blot with club soda to remove the stain, but you can also use milk to do the trick! All you have to do is pour it on, let it set, and give it time to soak and do its magic. Once the milk has had time to work, launder as usual, and watch that wine stain magically disappear. Although most milk will work, whole milk is the best stain fighter when it comes to wine.

- *Salt.* Salt has also been known to pick up wine spills, as well as grease. Try a mixture of salt and lemon juice to break down grease and rust stains. The lemon juice will break it down while the salt absorbs the stain.

- *Hydrogen peroxide.* Hydrogen peroxide not only removes stubborn baby formula stains, but also brightens yellowing white clothes. Apply a 50-50 mixture of cold water and hydrogen peroxide to battle the stain. Wait a bit until the stain is removed and air dry the garment to ensure the stain is gone. If the stain remains, try again with just peroxide and allow it to soak longer before washing. If the entire garment has yellowed, soak it in the peroxide/water mixture, then launder as usual.

Although these stain fighters really do work, it is important to understand that they came about out of sheer experimentation. The thing to do is to try attacking a stain from the easiest, cheapest, and greenest perspective. Before you buy expensive stain fighters, try using what you already have available to you in your home.

Whether you choose eco-friendly detergents, to allow the sun to dry your clothes, or just make the decision to wear more and wash less, the important thing to remember when greening your laundry is that trial-and-error efforts often produce productive, effective, and greener choices. Once you see what you can make happen with your own savvy sense and eager hands, you will be willing to give that extra effort to save money, energy, time, and the longevity of your favorite black pants.

Great Green Tip

Is your favorite, hand-knit sweater finally falling apart? Do you continue to wear it because you just can't give it up? Are you sentimentally connected to the person that made it for you? Don't worry. You don't have to get rid of it, or even donate it. Reuse it. Kiss that beautiful sweater good-bye and unravel it. Pull the yarn and collect it by rolling it into a ball. Return the yarn to the original creator. Not only will she be thrilled to have "new" yarn in her already busy hands, but once she sees how sad it makes you to lose that sweater, she may just make you a new hat, scarf, or gloves with the same yarn in order to keep that beloved sweater in your life.

Your Attic, Garage, and Basement: From Top to Bottom

44. Get Out of Hot Water

With nearly every major room in your house reinvented, or at least tweaked with a new green outlook, it is time to move on to some of the most overlooked areas for possible green makeovers: attics, garages, and basements.

Let's step into the garage for a moment. In some instances, you will find one of the main energy leeches in the house in your garage (and sometimes in your basement): the hot water heater. According to the U.S. Department of Energy, the hot water heater accounts for about 13 percent of your utilities. There are several ways to reduce the amount of energy used by a hot water heater:

Cut Back

One of the easiest and most obvious ways to avoid using as much energy is to cut back on your hot water use. We have already discussed taking shorter, cooler showers, and we have talked about using cold water when washing clothes. These are very efficient tips for saving money and energy when it comes to hot water heaters, but let's not forget that the hot water heater also feeds water to the dishwasher as well as all the faucets within the home. Washing dishes only when you have a full load, and deciding to use extremely hot water only when necessary rather than by preference will also greatly reduce your energy use and your water waste.

Lower the Temperature

Although most people prefer the option of having truly hot water, if the temperature on your hot water heater is set too high, it can scald your skin. According to the American Council for an Energy-Efficient Economy, for every 10°F lowered on a hot water heater, you can reduce heating costs by 3–5 percent. Try setting your hot water heater at 120°F. You will find this temperature not only efficient, but also comfortable as well.

Down the Drain

Drain some of the water from your hot water heater every now and then. Hot water heaters can collect sediment buildup that often causes them not to function properly. If you are unsure of how to do this, contact the manufacturer to ensure you are correctly maintaining the hot water heater, or check your instruction manual.

Make Wise Replacement Choices

When it is time to replace your hot water heater, you have a few options:

- Buy an energy-efficient labeled hot water heater. Doing so will ensure long-term savings.
- Consider a tankless hot water heater, which could amount to as much as a 30 percent difference when compared to a traditional natural gas storage tank heater.

- If you are ready for a change, try a solar hot water heater. According to the U.S. Department of Energy, installing a solar hot water heater could reduce carbon dioxide emissions by as much as 50 tons over a period of twenty years.

With the hot water heater working overtime in an average house, heating water for baths, dishwashers, showers, and washing machines, it only seems fair to give it a break every now and then. Take the time to make simple and green changes to avoid wasting money, energy, and valuable water. Choose to pull yourself from the hot water and make a greener choice for you and your overworked hot water heater.

45. Behind Closed Garage Doors

We may have covered the hot water heater, but we can't leave the garage without discussing what is usually in it. No, we aren't talking about the extra clothes bins for charity, the recycling waiting for a ride to the center, or the toys blocking the stairs and garage door. For some of us (not *us*, mind you), the garage isn't as much for storage as it is for housing your vehicle.

Don't worry! We aren't going to yell at you if you drive an SUV. How could we? We drive a compact SUV ourselves. Sure, gas is extremely expensive, and if you aren't using it for sports-related activities, towing, or anything more than a car can provide, then perhaps your SUV may be breaking you more than offering a cozy ride. We aren't saying that you have to get rid of your SUV, but we are suggesting a few greener, simple tricks that may help you drive smarter, rather than harder. Given our lifestyle and life choices, it is possible for one tank of gas to last us up to six weeks. How, you ask? There are several ways to make sure that you are getting the most from your vehicle (SUV or otherwise) while attempting to make greener and cleaner decisions for the environment.

Drive Less

If at all possible and permissible, try to leave your vehicle in the garage. When you need it, share it, or try to ride a bike, walk, or take public transportation. The more you leave the car behind, the more ingenious, resourceful, and free of it you will become.

Keep Up with Maintenance

A car is a system of working parts, and it is necessary to ensure that each part is properly working and not hampering the system. According to the EPA's Office of Mobile Sources, keeping your tires properly inflated can improve gas mileage, and you will get more life out of your tires when they are working at their best performance level. Make sure to balance and rotate your tires in accordance with your owner's manual to get the best quality and longevity. Check your fluids regularly, and keep up with oil changes. Make sure to keep your air filter in proper working order by replacing it when necessary. According to the government's fuel economy website, replacing a worn filter can improve gas mileage by as much as 10 percent. Basically, remember that a vehicle will perform to its fullest potential as long as you help it along. If you keep it well maintained, it can last for many years to come. Keeping up with maintenance can improve your gas mileage by as much as 40 percent.

Recycle Your Car

If you decide to tackle your own maintenance, make sure to properly dispose of fluids. If you change your own antifreeze, don't pour it on the ground, which can contaminate the soil as well as potentially poison children and pets. Make sure to take it to a service station or hazardous waste facility. If you replace a car battery, take it back to where you bought the new one to avoid any lead contamination.

According to the Environmental Defense Fund website, an estimated 2 to 3 billion tires already litter our land. To add to that, 240 million tires, potential fire hazards, are scrapped every year in the United States. When it is time to put on new tires, make sure to use a tire center or garage that will properly recycle your used tires. Some tire centers do recycle, and some do not. So, the responsibility is on your shoulders to ask. To find a tire center or service station in your area that will recycle your tires, go to earth911.org. Your recycled tires may, in fact, be the recycled landscape of your children's playground at school, daycare, or local parks.

When it is time to change the oil, make sure to take it to an oil-recycling center or to an Advance Auto Parts store or Autozone, or make sure to choose a service station that recycles oil.

Don't Buy More When You Can Use What You Have

The average amount of cars per household is 2.28. With single-car households at 34 percent of the market, and two-car households at 31 percent of the market, that leaves 35 percent owning three or more cars per household. Also, most vehicles are now designed to last up to 12 years or 128,500 miles. However, on average vehicles are being traded in or sold when they are only 4.5 years old with only 41,000 miles on them. It stands to reason that we, as a society, aren't using what we have effectively. Our obsession to have more, better, and flashier often gets the best of our egos and bank accounts. If you are already making a hefty car payment, don't upgrade, trade in, or try to sell when your car is already performing. Instead, make greener decisions with what you already have.

When Buying a New Car, Think About Your Needs

Remember, needs don't always match wants. If you are interested in an SUV, but will rarely use the extra space, four-wheel drive, or the basic sports orientation, perhaps a more fuel-efficient car is for you. Vehicles with more horsepower and heavier engines require more gas at the pump and you often get less gas mileage in the long run. Remember, buy only what you need, and completely use what you buy.

Of course, these are only a fraction of the ways to save money and make greener decisions when it comes to owning a vehicle, and we'll cover even more solutions later in the book. For now, just remember that you don't always have to get rid of the old and buy new. Drive what you have. Keep it maintained, and make sure to buy what suits your family's needs rather than what caters to your wants. Before you go into debt buying something new, try to green what you already have. Sometimes the best defense is to make smarter choices rather than more purchases.

Great Green Tip

Do you have several home projects waiting for your time, energy, and painting skills? Who doesn't have at least one gallon of paint lingering on the garage floor, waiting to be used, reused, or discarded? Before you trash those buckets in a garage-cleaning frenzy, check out the website earth911.org/re-cycling to find out how to judge your painting needs and pur-chases as well as how to properly dispose of or possibly recycle your paint. And, if you want some green bonus points, try buy-ing greener paints for your next household project.

46. Insulate Your Bank Account

If you are willing to battle the horror-movie images of gi-gantic, man-eating spiders and frightful apparitions waiting to attack your mind and inhabit your body, one of the most over-looked places for energy inefficiency can be your attic. When you venture into the attic, there are simple ways to ensure that you are properly insulated and that your bank account stays warm and snug.

The first line of defense in battling energy and heat loss is to take the time to check out your insulation. Those rows of pink are not only normal, but they are a welcome sight.

One of the easiest ways to decrease your energy bill and in-crease your energy efficiency is to simply add more insulation to what already exists. Unfortunately, that isn't as easy as it sounds. First, you must determine just how much you have and how thick your existing insulation already is. According to the U.S. Department of Energy, the easiest way to determine the type of insulation and the thickness is to measure behind an outlet. Turn off the power to the outlet, remove the cover and shine a flashlight onto the pink hugging the inside of your wall. Use a tape measure to gauge the thickness.

In order to better understand how much insulation you need, you have to determine the R-value (thermal resistance) of your insula-tion as well as how much is required or necessary for your area.

Basically, the higher the R-value, the more your heat stays in during the winter and the hot air stays at bay during the summer. However, unless you are an insulation technician, or a handy do-it-yourselfer with no inhibitions, this can be like reading a recipe for authentic Mexican salsa from a Greek cookbook. So, in order to better understand R-values, as well as find out what is appropriate for your neck of the woods, visit www.ornl.gov/sci to get a handle on your insulation needs.

Some other basics tips for conserving money and energy where your attic is concerned are:

- *Seal it up.* Seal any leaks in the attic with caulk or weather stripping to prevent heat loss or cold air from entering and leaving your heat working overtime to keep your home warm.
- *Keep out the clutter.* Sure, your attic is a great space for storage, but excessive clutter keeps air from circulating properly, especially through attic vents, and will prevent your attic from performing to its fullest potential.
- *Lock down the leaks.* Wet insulation from leaks can deteriorate or become moldy over time. It is necessary to make sure that your insulation is fully capable of keeping you cozy all year long.

Sure, you may only venture up there once a year to pull down the holiday decorations or to add a few more storage bins to the mix, but when you take that trip upstairs, check out your insulation to make sure your attic is functioning as greenly as possible—and keep your energy costs from leaving you out in the cold.

47. Your Green Foundation

Whether it is finished, carpeted, dirt, concrete, or wood, a basement can be one of the greatest places for children, sports equipment, home offices, or storage. Whether your basement is often used or rarely visited, there are ways to avoid losing energy and paying excess money. Overall, your basement experience can be more family oriented, more enjoyable, and more energy efficient by using the following simple tips:

- *Keep it covered.* In the winter, make sure to cover the windows of the basement with plastic to avoid excess cool air from entering. If you can, close the door and ensure your heat registers are closed when you aren't in there. This will avoid using excess heat to warm your basement. In the summer and spring, open the windows to allow natural light and circulating air to cool your basement area. Considering that your basement is the bottom floor, cool air should linger since only hot air rises.

- *Dry it out.* Make sure to keep your basement dry by attacking and eradicating any and all water leaks. If your basement tends to have standing water, you most likely have a foundation leak. According to the ENERGY STAR website, you can control foundation leaks by cleaning rain gutters and keeping the runoff away from the foundation as well as re-grading your soil to make sure that the ground slopes away from the foundation. Doing so will take water away from your basement rather than fill it.

- *Make it cozy.* If you have secured all leaks and have no water or mold issues, consider carpeting your basement. Adding carpet will keep those bare feet warmer, and it will help in keeping the basement cozy and toasty during winter months.

- *Condensation cure.* To reduce condensation during those hot, humid summer months, consider using a dehumidifier to keep your basement dry.

- *Dryer "do's."* If your dryer is located in the basement, make sure the dryer vent leads directly to the outside and is clear of obstruction. Doing so will increase your dryer's capability as well as conserve energy use.

- *Insulation information.* If you do not have insulation, you can add it to increase energy efficiency. However, there are advantages and disadvantages to doing so, and you may want to visit www.eere.energy.gov/consumer before making the decision to change the insulation in your basement.

- *Turn it off.* If you have office equipment or any appliances that use electrical outlets, make sure to turn it off before leaving the basement. That goes for space heaters, fans, lights, or media equipment. Most often, if it is out of sight, it is out of mind. Give yourself peace of mind and energy savings by turning off all equipment before coming upstairs. And make sure to unplug anything that could suck energy away from under your watchful eyes.

Whether you choose to entertain in your basement or to use it for excess storage room, make sure to check and double check it for all potential energy leaks. Doing so will ensure that your energy bill doesn't get the best of you and that your green house will be built from the foundation up. Taking the time to check your basement, attic, and garage will not only ensure that you are getting the absolute most out of your money, but also that your home is firmly built with green roots and sturdy branches.

Great Green Tips

Although the garage often harbors your vehicle or tools, often-times you also use your garage for your pet's storage items as well. Next to your tools, broom, and charity bins, make sure to have natural pet-care products rather than chemical-laced ones, a leash to keep your dog neighbor friendly, natural kitty litter to avoid using clay-based litter, tags and shot records for your animal, and healthy food for its needy belly. Along with taking green care of your pet, remember to try to adopt or take in animals in need of homes rather than searching for high-priced, pure-bred animals. A furry friend is a friend, be it from the animal shelter next door or the abandoned pet "drop-off" parking lot down the street. Reusing and recycling doesn't always have to be about trash, tires, or rainwater. If a pet needs a home, and you have a home, take the time to become fast, green friends.

Are you sleeping in the same dent that has held your body for years? Sure, you already vacuum your mattress to keep dust mites away, but have you considered moving it to keep your body comfortable and lovingly snuggled? Take the time to rotate your mattress. Not only will you find a new, comfortable niche previously unexplored, but you will also ensure that you are getting the best possible use from your mattress. Taking the time to use it and reuse it as long as it will allow keeps you sleeping in your mattress snug as a bug in a rug.

When a baby is in the house, your entire world revolves around ensuring that baby is getting the best of everything: care, cuddling, and food. Sure, you can always buy healthy food in those baby food jars, but why not cut the cost and waste and create your own baby food? Harvest from your garden, steam that broccoli or squash, puree it, and feed it to your sweet cherub! When you want to store it, all you have to do is spoon it out into a divided ice cube tray, seal it in a freezer bag, and put it away until time to thaw. This creates a fantastic individual serving, and you aren't throwing out those baby food jars! When you have a baby, face it, every saved penny is welcome.

Tired of all the shuffled papers in your life? Step out from your paper piles and take control! Consider moving your banking online. Or, if you feel comfortable with the idea, consider having your bills automatically deducted from your account. Managing paperwork is hard enough. Take some of the pressure off yourself and put it on your computer. You will save paper, envelopes, and money on stamps!

We all love entertainment. Who doesn't enjoy a good movie or a relaxing CD after a long day at work? It is wonderful to let loose and allow your mind to relax. But, when the movie gets old, or you are tired of the music, what do you do with the DVDs and CDs lying about? Exchange them! Just like that toy exchange with your kids' friends, set up an adult one with yours! Or, if you don't feel comfortable trading, consider selling them at a store. There are countless stores for buying and selling used movies or CDs. All you have to do is open your phonebook and find them.

PART THREE
Nurture the Green Genes

*F*un, crafty, and educational ways to plant green seeds of change in our children.*

No matter the mountains climbed, the roads traveled, or the work accomplished, little compares to when a new baby first enters the world. From the moment you hold the tiny bundle in your arms, the child becomes the reason for your dreams, goals, and future decisions. But, alongside those heartwarming smiles and proud parent ramblings comes the scary realization that you are immediately responsible for another person's health and future.

You may think that first diaper is daunting (and it is!), but nothing really packs a punch as much as those first questions of "Why?" followed by the fear and realization that your child is looking to you, the adult, for the answers. That is when it really starts to hit you: complete panic. What if your answers are wrong? Unethical? Unfounded? Ridiculous? Although it is always fun to turn the questions back to the child, and quite often it does produce interesting answers, at some point you have to be willing to take the reigns and guide your child into adulthood.

Now, are we the parenting experts? Absolutely, one hundred percent, not! However, what we have begun to realize about parenthood is that not only do we have the chance to explain and encourage, but also the responsibility to instill in our children that it is important to stand up and do something when a change needs to be made. And, better yet, if we take the time to listen to their points of view, their innocent view of the world, and their ideas for change, we just may learn something from them. So, without further ado . . . this one is for the kids.

48. Chat with Those Chatty Critters

If you have or know any children at all, one of the things you are well aware of is the lack of silence. Whether you are shopping, reading, playing, or even sleeping, there is never a moment of complete silence when children are around. And, if you have had, been around, or know any children around the ages of three or four, one of the things you are most accustomed to is the ever-dreaded and always-abundant question of "Why?" It is continuous and relentless.

If you have ever taken the time to listen to your little tot at play, one thing that you begin to realize is that they are and have been, listening to your answer. Not only are they listening, but they are repeating. And regurgitating to their friends, neighbors, and grandparents. The thing to remember about those prying and perky ears is that you have the power to have meaningful green conversations that plant the seeds for your child to help the environment in the future. And you can expect them, with their innocent love for you, to believe what you tell them. So tell it truthfully, and greenly! The one constant between adults and children is that they are always watching and listening. It is up to us to teach, answer, and guide them.

Take the time to discuss green issues with your children. Ask them what it means to recycle, and listen to their answers. Once you open the dialogue, you will find great green-teaching opportunities at every turn, thus setting them up to one day lead the world in making solid, environmentally friendly choices. Discuss littering and how that negatively impacts our world. Explain the need to turn off lights when they leave a room and to turn off the water while they brush their teeth. Talk about the need to reuse and reduce. Involve them in green family decisions, and take the time to explain why trees are important to our world and to our fragile ecosystems. Every time you make the choice to create a conversation, you are showing your child that discussion and open dialogue are the first courses of action toward a global understanding and a unified front against the environmental problems facing our world. And you are teaching them that it is their world, too, and that their opinions, their decisions, and most importantly, their actions will ultimately determine the future of our Earth.

As parents, we are the most influential people in their lives. Taking the time for conversation with children is the first, and most important, way to make a positive green impact in their lives. Put your best green foot forward and talk to them about recycling, pollution, and how to implement green choices into your family life. Once you take that first step, positive actions will most certainly follow.

49. Green Creations

Whether you're a parent, an aunt or uncle, a grandparent, or a childcare provider, chances are you will be challenged with the task of keeping a fidgeting child entertained. Sure, you can always turn on the television or hand them a handheld video game, but if you want a chance to save electricity, allow their imaginations to run wild, and find a teachable green moment, why not try crafting with them instead? You don't have to be crafty to craft. And you don't have to search craft stores for expensive materials, either. Everything you need is right in your home, even if it's not obvious at first.

Here are a few green crafts to get you started.

Green Placemats
Brown paper shopping bag
Crayons
Magazines
Markers
Clear contact paper
Scissors
Glue
Old photographs

1. Cut the paper bag to desired placemat size.
2. Help kids cut out interesting pictures from magazines, or allow them to color on the bag. Marker on it. Glue on it. Make family collages with leftover photographs. The point is to allow the kids to use their imaginations in any way they wish.

3. Once the decorating is finished and the glue is dry, cover the placemat with contact paper, and cut edges into whatever designs strike your fancy.

That's it! The wonderful thing about this project is that it takes the work from your hands and puts it all into theirs. They will love their new placemats, which, in turn, gets them to the table a bit quicker when it comes time for dinner.

Fridge Poetry
Magazines
Scissors
Clear contact paper
Magnetic tape

1. Help the kids cut out interesting words or phrases from the magazines.
2. Cover the words with contact paper, and trim the edges to just around the ends of the words.
3. Add magnetic tape to the back to create fridge magnets.

Once you have the words ready to put on the fridge, watch as your fledgling poet begins to spread his creative wings. Kids have endless fun with this, and you may find yourself standing in front of the fridge, making a little poetry yourself. It is also a fun and nifty way to leave messages for other family members.

Recycled Greeting Cards
We all get our share of greeting cards, especially around the holidays, and it is always nice to know that someone out there is thinking of you. However, once you have that card and have dis-

played it for a few days, what's next? Do you throw it away? The simple green answer is obviously to recycle. Ah, but the crafty green answer is to reuse it!

Old greeting cards
Brown paper bags
Scissors
Glue
Markers, stamps, glitter, lace, or fabric

1. Allow the kids to choose a card of their liking.
2. When a card has been chosen, help them cut the front graphic away from the rest of the card. Make sure to put the other "used" portion of the card in the recycling bin. Or, if you prefer a sturdier backing, cut a brown paper bag to the size of the card and glue it to the inside. Once you have glued it in place, you will have a "clean slate" to write on.
3. If you prefer to only use the front graphic, cut the paper bag to the appropriate size for a card, and fold it like a card.
4. Glue the graphic onto the front.
5. Allow the kids to marker, glue, glitter, lace, or stamp it however they choose. Help write a personalized message inside.
6. Put it in an envelope and mail it out for any holiday or occasion imaginable. If you want to get really crafty, consider making the envelope out of another brown paper bag!

Sure, it isn't glossy and new, but it is personal, handmade, recycled, and constructive. And that beats spending more money for a greeting card any day. You really don't need kids to take this green tip to the greeting card bank. Reuse old greeting cards, and create your own masterpieces to send out for holidays or thoughtful occasions.

Green Paper Dolls

Looking for something to do with all of those clothing catalogs that clutter your mailbox each day? Try giving them a new purpose before you recycle them. Have you ever noticed that people stand in similar poses in clothing catalogs? In this project, that will work to your child's advantage *and* imagination.

What you will need:

Catalog
Scissors
Clear contact paper
Magnetic tape

1. Cut out models from the catalog, and then search for clothing being modeled by another model in a similar pose. This way, you are sure to have more of a "fit" for your dolls.
2. Once your child has a sufficient amount of clothes, shoes, coats, hats, and whatever other accessory she may enjoy, cover them with contact paper and trim them so that they can be interchanged. Place magnetic tape on the back of the dolls as well as the clothing to allow them to stick to a fridge or blackboard.
3. Mix and match to create hours of paper doll magic.

Of course, the clothes won't fit perfectly like the store-bought version, but the beauty of a child's imagination is that they will never see the difference. They will become so absorbed with their own set of paper dolls that they will never care or realize that the shirt doesn't fit exactly over the doll's arms. They will just be happy to play, imagine, and create their own toy.

Green Flash Cards

Do you have a developing reader on your hands? Try creating your own flash cards to make the process educational, fun, and interactive. Not only will you have fun creating them, but you will also make sure that your children get hands-on experience connecting objects with words rather than just trying to sound out a word with no tangible object attached.

What you will need:

Junk mail, magazines, catalogs, broken or torn books
Scissors
Clear contact paper

1. Cut out any and all words that can be attached to objects throughout your home.
2. Cover them with contact paper and trim them.
3. Attach them to the corresponding object.

The fun part about this is that your children create their own educational learning tool and will learn how to read without the help of computers, electronic books, or hairy animals on the television. Whether you choose to be the one pointing out the words, or you allow your children to wander on their own, connecting letters and words with objects they have learned to recognize, they will be learning while they play, recycle, and turn off the electronics!

Dry-Erase Doodle Pages

Brown paper bag or a sheet of paper
Clear contact paper
Dry-erase markers

1. Cover the paper with contact paper and trim to desired size.
2. Use the dry-erase markers to draw, erase, and draw again.

This is one of the quickest and easiest ways to solve the problem of your little artist constantly needing another sheet of paper. Rather than despair over the wastefulness of young Van Gogh–in–the-making, create a green reusable solution that will keep your artists entertained without stunting their budding artistic desires. Once they draw, erase, and draw again, they will be thrilled with their new doodle page. When it begins to lose its luster, simply create a new one. These doodle pages won't last forever, especially with young, eager hands working with them. But why go through hundreds of pieces of paper the old-fashioned way when you can whittle that down to just a few?

Green Shopping List
Scissors
Piece of cardboard box or cereal box
Magazines, newspapers, or coupon sections
Clear contact paper
Velcro strips
*Markers, stickers, glitter, feathers (or anything else your child
      would enjoy using for decorations)*

1. Cut out pictures of food or any other items on your grocery list.
2. Cover each picture completely with contact paper to make sure it can be used more than once.
3. Place one strip of the Velcro on the cardboard or cereal box and the other on the back of the picture.
4. Ask each child to personalize his or her list with the glitter, markers, or whatever makes him or her happy.
5. Attach list items to the cardboard or cereal box.
6. Rotate items on the list for each grocery visit.

Every child loves to feel needed. Giving children a job and their own personalized shopping list will keep them occupied while you shop, but most importantly, they will be happy to have a list that they created with their own hands. And, as a family, you will have recycled as well as found a new craft to do on rainy days.

Once you take the time to start looking for green crafting fun, you will find that you can create a multitude of green projects throughout your home. Of course, crafting isn't for everyone. But, when you are searching for something to do that doesn't require electricity, money, or a large amount of effort, these crafts can prove enjoyable and educational for most kids. Not only will you be keeping them occupied, but they will also be learning fundamental green ideas such as recycling, reusing, and reducing electrical energy use as they go. Who knew green learning could be so deceptively fun?

Great Green Tip

Take the guesswork out of shopping for gifts for young babies and toddlers. Rather than trying to find that perfect toy, try donating money to plant trees in the child's name. Visit the Arbor Day Foundation at www.arborday.org or the American Forests website at www.americanforests.org/planttrees or the Tree Fund website at www.treefund.org for a permanent reminder of your affection. Still want to give a wrapped gift? Pull a box from your recycling bin, wrap it in old paper bags, decorate it, and be the hit of the party. The recipient is guaranteed to crawl in, climb on, hide in, and adore it. And you will be doing the Earth some good as well.

50. Toy with It

From the moment children are old enough to see color and shapes, they become fascinated with the toy aisle at the store. Bright colors attract them, music entrances them, and flashing lights enrapture them. With all the options out there, and all the toys overflowing in most closets, how can you avoid the trap of those pleading, puppy dog eyes while you try to venture through the store? Of course, as you may have already guessed, there is a green answer. Actually, there are several of them!

Considering that your child will always have birthdays, not to mention very persuasive pleading abilities, there are other ways to ensure that your child is not simply buying into the urge to have more and use less. Here are a few green options for toys.

Buy Less

Kids don't need as much as they want. Really, do any of us? We all have a tendency to have way too much in our closets, and that usually goes for kids as well. The less they have, the more they will play with what they do have, and the more they will appreciate it.

Store More

One of the greatest things about kids is that if it is out of sight, then it is out of mind. You can pack several unopened or unused or gently used toys into a storage bin, and they will never realize their stash has been halved. So, when it comes time for new toys, take a few out of the bin, and then add a few old ones to it. They will be thrilled with their "new" toy, and this ensures that each toy gets quality time rather than being tossed aside. When the time comes to rotate again, that old toy that has been stored for a few months will seem brand new again.

Buy Secondhand

When a child is young, it is the toy that matters, not the package. Many secondhand stores, yard sales, or friendly neighbors have fantastic nearly new toys that can go from their hands to your child's. Giving a toy a second life will decrease waste and will increase savings.

Exchange It

Set up a toy exchange with your kids' friends. Have you ever noticed that your child relishes the experience of playing at a friend's house? Even if your child has the same toy at home, you will find your child entranced by the friend's version. Of course, you do need to set up an exchange with friends with the understanding that you only use toys that would be okay if they get broken, lost, or whatever else little hands can accomplish. Toys do get painted, smashed, and misplaced, so if you do exchange with a friend, make sure not to swap Junior's favorite toy. The best way to ensure that all toys are accounted for is to create a list of exchange toys. Cover it with clear contact paper and use dry-erase markers to keep track of which family has which toy. This way you will get the most use out of the toy, and you will ensure that all exchange toys are circulating and being played with. And, if you find your child isn't as interested as originally expected, you always have the option to trade again. That wonderful advantage doesn't exist with store-bought impulse toys.

Buy Locally

With so many toy recalls in the news lately, why not support local products instead? Search local craft fairs, artists, and toy stores for toys made by your neighbors and friends. Buying from local toy-makers will not only ensure your product is locally made, but also will pour your money into the local economy. Sure, they may be more expensive, but if they are handmade, isn't it worth putting your money into your neighborhood rather than thousands of miles away?

Charge It

Buying and installing batteries is one of the more expensive aspects of having children. One thing you can definitely expect from a color-ful, new toy from the toy store is that it comes with lights, bells, and whistles. The first way to avoid wasting money, and more en-ergy, is to avoid using batteries whenever possible. If your child never knows about the flashing lights and true-to-life train whistle, then he or she may never really care.

Given that batteries have become handy in our everyday uses of cameras, toys, and remotes, it has become normal to throw them away when they get weak or die. However, when you look at the composition of a basic AA, AAA, C, or D battery, most of them are composed of heavy metals such as mercury, cadmium, lead, and nickel. According to the Environmental Health and Safety website, in the United States alone, about 3 billion batteries are sold every year, averaging 32 per family.

Those little batteries that we are all used to are actually very power-ful chemically, and what we may not realize is that the heavy metals from our batteries wind up in landfills, where they contaminate and pollute the environment. These batteries:

- Pollute lakes and streams through harmful vapors caused by the incineration process.
- May potentially leach heavy metals while decomposing in a landfill.
- Expose land and water to lead and acid.
- Allow mercury to vaporize when burned, and wind up in the air; cadmium and lead may stay behind in the leftover ash.

Not only do these issues pose environmental concerns for the land, but they could also make their way up the food chain through polluting the water supply, which would eventually lead to animal exposure. So, rather than throw away those batteries when they run low in your child's toy, make sure to contact your local recycling center to find out how to properly dispose of them. If you need help finding your local center, visit earth911.org to get started.

Although rechargeable batteries also contain heavy metals and should be recycled or properly disposed of as well, each rechargeable battery used equates to hundreds of one-time-use batteries over the course of its life. Of course, they are more expensive upfront, and they often require buying a charger; however, given the green benefit of using and reusing as opposed to buying and tossing, if you use a lot of batteries in your home, going with rechargeables may be much more efficient and greener in the long run.

Although kids will always want toys, and we will always buy toys for them, there are greener ways to approach it. The younger our children are when they start learning to use and reuse, as well as to buy less rather than buy more and later discard, the more these lessons will stick with them throughout their lives. Sure, they may always want more, but when they start to realize that they really don't have to have more to be happy, they will appreciate what's in their closets more and more. And those early lessons will stay with them for the rest of their lives. The toys may get bigger, but the intrinsic lessons remain the same. After all, it is about using and reusing what we already have.

51. Put the F-U-N Back in the Family Functions

When kids are small, there is no one cooler than their parents. However, when they hit those dreadful tween years, their parents turn into alien life forms who must be avoided at all cost. Whether they run to you or from you, one thing that resonates with every child, young and old, is quality time spent. Who doesn't like being the center of attention? And don't all adults have fond memories of some elder taking the time to play, laugh, walk, or just spend a few minutes of quality time with them? One of the greatest and greenest ways to connect with your children is to have a family fun day outside.

With video games enticing them, television calling them, cell phones ringing them, and portable DVD players entertaining them, it can be very hard to convince a modern child to venture into the great outdoors. But once you hold a family fun day outdoors, they will become not only addictive, but also extremely family productive. In case you need a few ideas to get you started:

Go Fly a Kite

Of course you need a little help from the wind, and a small amount of practice and skill to get it in the air, but kids, tall or small, always love flying kites. For extra green points, while you are all staring into the wild blue yonder, searching for the tail of your soaring kite, take the time to have a conversation about pollution, smog, and air quality.

Take a Hike

You can always decide to take a long nature hike out in the woods, taking the time to hear the birds, feel the wind, and listen to the distant babbling brook. It is soothing and healthy, and it gets your family moving, listening, and talking. If you prefer the concrete jungle to the green forest floor, try taking a nature hike around your neighborhood. Take a jar or mesh container, and watch as your child becomes the insect hunter, eager to track that elusive caterpillar or slithery lizard. Kids love exploring, and you can take the opportunity to explain nature, the balance of sustainable living, and the local ecosystems thriving and needing protection, all in your very own neighborhood whether that be suburb, concrete, or country hillsides.

Plant and Sustain Your Garden

The easiest and greenest way to teach your children about replenishing as well as not wasting is to allow them to plant, maintain, harvest, and eat their own fruits and vegetables. You will be amazed at what children will try, and often like, if they know it came from their own nurturing hands. In doing so, perhaps they will obtain a better understanding about the amount of food we tend to waste every day. In 2006, municipal solid waste generation was 251 million tons. The food scraps contribution of that number roughly was 12.4 percent—that's approximately 31 million tons of wasted food. We can reduce that through showing our kids how to properly and healthily portion our food as well as eat all that is on the plate. Along the way, you have a teachable moment to discuss farming, natural weeding remedies, ecosystems, and the very real issue of casual waste in this country. Once a child has the opportunity to see where food comes from, and has had the chance to actually cultivate it, the child will better understand the need to eat what is taken and to take only what will be eaten.

Go to McDonald's

McDonald's farm, that is! If you just don't trust your own gardening skills or don't have the space to garden, take the kids to the source of all our food. Visit a local farm or an orchard, and arrange to take a tour. Take the time to learn about the farming techniques of your local farmers. Are they free-range farmers? Do they practice organic techniques? Do they use pesticides? Finding out exactly what goes into your food (or on it) is not only educational, but also healthy. Kids will enjoy the chance to pet, feed, or just watch the animals in action. And, they may get the opportunity to harvest, and eat, apples from a beautiful orchard.

Make Like a Tree and Leave

Whether you go to the park, play in your own backyard, or simply encourage your children to play an outdoor sport, make sure to get them outside into the world that not only sustains them, but also keeps them healthy as well.

No matter how you spend family fun day, you can take steps to make it as green as possible. Making and participating in green activities as a family opens the lines of communication as well as provides teachable moments for greener living. Just talking about a greener lifestyle will go in your children's ears and immediately ooze out of them. Being actively engaged in green activities as well as leading by example is the best, and greenest, policy when it comes to planting those green seeds in their growing genes.

Great Green Tip

Unsure of what to get that newly expecting couple? Forget expensive baby clothes, swings, cribs, or bouncing seats. Instead of buying something new, collect gently used baby gear. You can always find spare baby gadgets and paraphernalia at second-hand stores, yard sales, or even from your cousin's nephew's wife.

Or you can give them a gift that *really* matters: Make them a book of babysitting coupons. When they have been up for days, listening to a crying baby and pacing the floors, they won't care about that expensive pink jumper! What they will care about is someone who will provide babysitting services free of charge. Save a lot of money, reuse nearly new baby gear, and help those new parents in need when it really matters most!

52. Take 'Em Along for the Ride

You can talk the talk, but until you walk the walk, kids won't fully understand the reason or necessity for the green choices or decisions you are making for them. One of the easiest ways to walk that walk is to allow the kids to walk it with you. Before they can truly understand the difference that they are making in this world through greener decisions, they have to fully see the process from the conception to the clean-up.

Although there are a few obvious green outings such as going to farms and orchards, and hiking, there are also green opportunities that are more obscure and overlooked.

Check It Out

One of the greatest examples of a green community is your local library. Kids love the story time that is usually offered at most libraries, and they also enjoy the process of choosing a book and using their very own library card. Although this may not seem like a green experience for them, what they are learning by going to the library with you is that books do not always have to be bought—they can be borrowed or shared. Take the time to take your kids to the library and to teach them that for each book bought new, there are trees that had to offer up their gems. Explain the printing process, how the paper is used, as well as the importance of using recycled paper. You will find that they treasure those library books because they know they have the option of returning them and checking out more to their heart's content. For extra green points, try creating your own children's library within your circle of friends. Allow your children to check out a friend's collection while sharing some of their own.

Head to the Recycling Center

One of the coolest things about recycling centers is that they are very open to allowing your children or groups of children in for tours to learn more about the importance of recycling. This is a truly fun experience for kids because they have the chance to go through the process from beginning to end. Go through your recycling with your children. Allow them to sort, clean, decide upon, and collect various items throughout the house that can be either reused or taken to the recycling center. Then, take those items to the center and ask for a tour of the plant. Make sure to take the time to tour with the children, find out some interesting facts yourself, and then sit back and watch as their inner wheels start turning. From there, move on to the store where the kids can take the time to pick out re-cycled paper towels, cereal boxes, and paper. Allowing them to par-ticipate and witness the full circle of recycling will solidify their desire to take action. The children will be proud that they are doing something so productive, and they will be learning and practicing what you have been talking and preaching.

Get Hands-on

Kids know and appreciate action. Get them involved in the process of sorting through toys and clothes to give to charity. Allow them to go through toys, clothes, shoes, coats, and even socks. When they realize that they are doing something very real and productive in helping others in need, you will find that they will begin to ac-tively search for things to give away. Knowing and seeing that other little boys and girls are happy with their "new" things are power-ful incentives and motivational fuel for your children.

Once they have gathered their belongings to give to charity, take them with you to give them away. They will be proud of themselves, and you will be proud of them. Make sure to finish that process by practicing what you preach. Buy secondhand. Take them with you to the secondhand stores, and explain that other little boys and girls have given these clothes and toys for them to love and enjoy. Teaching them that clothes and toys can be passed along to oth-ers will ensure that they learn the need to use and reuse, and you will have brought the entire process around full circle.

Be a Repairing Pair

One of the best ways to ensure that your kids are learning how to take care of their things is to help them understand that if it is broken, they can fix, repair, restitch, or even glue it back together. This may seem obvious, but when you repair a toy or a piece of clothing for them, rather than allowing them to be a part of it, they begin to assume that taking care of their things is someone else's job. So, one of the best ways to teach children to reuse something until it can't be used anymore is to take them through the process of lovingly repairing it.

Allow them to get involved in restitching their favorite toys and stuffed animals or their favorite pair of holey jeans. Ask them to pick out fun and colorful patches to cover the holes. Not only will they be excited to have "new" clothes, but also to have been involved in the process of making them "new" again. Also, get your kids involved in fixing their broken bicycles, toys, stuffed animals, games, and anything else that just needs a little TLC. Taking the time to show your kids that items don't necessarily have to be tossed, but can be lovingly renewed, is a surefire way to ensure that they learn to appreciate what they have, use it fully, and then make the decision to either cut it up for spare rags, or finally toss it when no life is left to it.

Fill Their Minds

Although it may not seem like the most fun family adventure, taking a trip to a landfill can be a very eye-opening experience. Talking to your children may help them understand the need for recycling, but until they see the massive mound of trash in a landfill, they will not have a true understanding of the importance of conserving. It isn't appetizing, and it definitely isn't appealing, but once you take the time to check one out, you have the chance to break into discussions about littering, the need for recycling, landfill processes, leaching chemicals, and countless other environmental and people issues. Seeing it all firsthand, and witnessing the real difference that picking up litter, recycling, and reusing can make will solidify greener choices in your child's mind.

Water Their Minds

If you take the time to visit your local water treatment plant so your children can witness the process your water must go through before it passes your lips, they will be more interested in preserving and protecting that valuable supply. Discuss with your children the need to conserve water and reduce pollution in our waterways as well as ways to protect and ensure them for the future.

Whether or not you make the decisions for the household, one of the most important things to remember is that if you want your kids to make and create real green changes in their world, you have to let them get onboard and take that green cruise with you. Talking about all these things will create an avenue for change, but allowing them to discuss, question, and most importantly, take action alongside you will be the key to ensuring that your kids will carry your green hopes and ideals into the next generation.

53. Too Green for School

For those of you who have been away from the school bus or the classroom for a while and your children aren't old enough for school yet, take the time to dig into your sensory reserve and remember the excitement and squealing (not to mention begging) involved in the annual "school supplies" shopping trip. There is nothing better than the smell of glue or a new box of crayons!

Of course, buying school supplies always means searching for the perfect color, character, and brand name. However, along with those fantastic standards of scissors, pencil boxes, and backpacks come toxins, virgin-fiber use, and nonrenewable resource use. Americans spent $14.1 billion on back-to-school supplies (in 2003). That statistic supports the idea that when it comes to school supplies, it's definitely worth exploring green options and considering a green makeover for your children's schooling experience.

Here are some ways to green intervene with your children's school supplies.

Reuse

If there's one word that bears repeating, it's "reuse." Sure, kids want new and popular supplies, but sometimes, used and close to perfect will oddly be good enough. If you do have old school supplies or clothes that still fit the bill, don't cave in and buy new ones when the old ones will still do. Before you go out and buy absolutely everything new, take the time to shop secondhand stores as well as go through last year's school supplies of a friend, family member, or neighbor. You will be surprised how often your children will go for it, especially when it comes from someone they know and love. If your children just won't let up, and you are feeling sorry for them, then set a certain amount of new purchases to go along with last year's supply. Sometimes just giving your children a small amount of elbow room will prevent the dreaded in-store meltdown.

Go Green

If you are buying new supplies for your children, why not go green? Along with those traditional school supplies, you can now find affordable, green options for your children such as recycled paper, pencil boxes, pencils, and even backpacks. So, before you buy what you are used to seeing, double check the aisle and look for that friendly recycled symbol.

Get Involved

If you have kids in school already, chances are you are as involved in their schooling as you can possibly be. But, rather than just attending the functions or becoming a familiar face at parent–teacher meetings, try to find out more about your children's in-school recycling options, green energy choices, book-sharing possibilities, food waste policies, school/local lunch relationships, and recess and outdoor interaction. Getting involved in your children's green school options will not only show your interest and concern, but it will also teach them that if a change can be made, a chance has to be taken. Taking the time to research the school, get involved in greener options, and take the initiative to start them when possible will teach your children how to get involved and how to make their school experience a green experience.

Take a Stroll

If you live within the vicinity of your children's school, and if time permits, try walking with them to school. If that isn't an option, check out your school's bus situation. According to the Union of Concerned Scientists website, the average school bus is responsible for twice as much soot pollution per mile as that of a tractor-trailer truck. And the kids onboard are breathing it in. However, many school districts are making great efforts to address this problem. Hybrid buses are making a debut as well as buses running on vegetable oil, but it will be some time before all school systems have the capability to use them. Before you put your little one on a bus, take the time to research and learn about your local busing system. You may find a green bus option, or you may realize that the convenient route isn't necessarily the greenest route. A greener option is to carpool to the school: Get with a friend, or three friends, and take turns taking each other's kids to school. Not only will this save gas and reduce the amount of cars on the road, but it will also give you a day or two off a week to just sit back, relax, and fully enjoy your breakfast before starting your day.

Green Lunches

When making the decision about whether your children should eat at school or pack their own lunches, check out the greener options available today. Some schools are developing programs that offer locally grown food options for lunch. There are eco-friendly lunchboxes available now as well as lunch bags. If you do send your children with their lunch, consider packing reusable silverware as well as food containers. The disposable, one-time-use food containers and lunches are convenient, but they are producing more waste rather than reusing. And, rather than go for the one-time-use drink boxes, go retro and send them with a thermos or even provide them with a reusable aluminum bottle to hold their favorite beverages. The idea is to remove the eat-and-trash trend and replace it with the eat-reuse-reduce green method. Not only will you reduce the amount of trash your children go through, but you will also save money by making fewer purchases rather than weekly or daily purchases for food or drinks that will only hit the trash bin.

Back-to-school time is always exciting for both parents and students. Go ahead and enjoy that back-to-school shopping trip. However, before you head out, take the time to inventory what you already have, and to make a list of potential green choices that both you and your children intend to make. Not only will you set a green goal for your children, but you will also be setting a green example for them as well as their curious friends.

Great Green Tip

Do you find it hard to throw away your children's favorite toys, clothes, or shoes? Then don't. Take pieces of their favorite things and turn them into personal mementos. Use pieces of their baby clothing as quilting fabric. Create Christmas decorations for your tree or holiday gifts for your family by using shoes, toys, stuffed animals, or images from your children's favorite books. Create holiday cards from their used and tattered books, or create and frame a collage of their favorite bedtime stories. Taking the time to find new uses for what would otherwise hit the trash can will reduce your waste, increase your memories, and help you avoid buying expensive decorations. Why buy something new when you can fill your home with loving, gorgeous memories?

54. Let Them Take the Reins

With energy-conserving family discussions, trips to the landfill, recycled crafting projects, and green school shopping under your belt, there couldn't be any more to add, right? Wrong. One of the most important aspects of greening your kids' genes is to allow them to venture out into the world and to see how their green ideas and goals can immediately affect their environment. Although they may have already discussed greener choices and become involved in the family green forum, allowing them to branch out on their own to actually put their green theories into practice is not only necessary in order for them to perpetuate real change, but it is also important to allow them to feel pride and responsibility, and to see firsthand what their own hands can do to create positive change for this world.

Here are a few ideas to get them started:

- *Take action.* One of the easiest and greenest ways to make a difference in your neighborhood is to simply pick up the litter. Grab a trash bag and some rubber gloves and help your children set a powerful example of responsibility for neighborhood friends. If you want to go that extra green mile, the Keep America Beautiful foundation is one of the best ways to get their hands dirty, and to get them involved in helping to clean up their own local area.

- *Get educated.* Although the job of a parent or caregiver is to educate, you can bet that the majority of your children's education will come about outside the home. One of the best ways to ensure that education is green and soundly grounded in Earth-friendly values is to get them involved with outdoor programs. Try avenues such as 4H camp to learn about practical and life experience, recreational camp to get them in touch with the benefits and joys of their world, or the Boy or Girl Scouts to teach them how to survive in, correctly benefit from, or replenish this Earth. Along with saving our environment, get them involved in saving their neighborhoods and communities. One of the most productive and immediately satisfying ways to learn about community, togetherness, and the strength found in unified hands is through Habitat for Humanity. Kids can work together with friends, neighbors, or family members to build a home for a needy family. Not only will working with Habitat for Humanity teach children about the need to reach out and lend a helping hand, but it will also provide an opportunity to watch local workers, volunteers, and families working together to create a difference and to put their efforts into their local community. Allowing them to focus on how to actively and greenly live and work together to create change in this world will instill the desire in them to tend and correctly maintain the Earth for the duration of their lives.

● *Ask them for help*. One of the greatest ways to get children involved is to ask them what they would do. So, although you are making green choices for the family, allow them to suggest and implement a green change, too. When children take the time to research, suggest, and take control of a decision, follow their ideas and lead. This could be as simple as deciding that each member of the family must remember to turn off the light when leaving a room. Each violator may be required to put change in a family money jar that must be used in a green or environmentally friendly way. Whatever the children come up with, encourage it and follow through with it in order to show that the ideas and input are valuable both to you and to the future of our world.

Whether it be through putting them in the middle of family discussions or allowing them to branch out through community service or outdoor survival skills, allowing your children to take charge of their own green lives will ensure that they put their best green feet forward and become active citizens who will not only lend a hand, but will also push to do the work themselves. The children truly are the future, and they need to know and be aware of what faces them in the world. More importantly, they need to know how their hands can actively and productively create change that will benefit not only their generation, but also the generations of their children and grandchildren as well.

Looking for a unique, personalized gift for someone? Consider making and giving a bookmark.

Here's what you need:

Leftover family pictures
Scissors
Glue stick
Brown shopping bag
Clear contact paper

1. Sift through your old, candid photos and cut and create a collage of your family. They don't have to be perfect pictures, so don't worry about finding the best shot you have of little Junior's recital.
2. Use the glue stick to attach your photos to the brown bag. Create whatever shape you would like in your final bookmark.
3. When the glue dries, cover the photo collage with the contact paper, and trim it to the desired shape.

Voilà! You have successfully created a personalized bookmark for that special someone. Not only will you avoid throwing away those scrap pictures, but also share special family moments with someone else.

PART FOUR
Work It

Simple ways to maintain your input and recycle your output at work.

Although it can be fun to hang out with kids all day long, it is also important and necessary to address the joys and thrills that can come about from work. The daily grind often consists of pushing ourselves from the bed, gulping down our morning coffee, and rushing out the door, only to be met with other rushing workers and mind-numbing traffic jams. Although work may be necessary, there are greener ways to make it to work, make it through work, and make it more environmentally friendly when you do finally clock out for the day.

You may be wondering what could possibly make your work day greener, especially when your work revolves around nothing environmental. Although it may be hard to make significant green changes such as changing all energy power to green energy power within your building, it is possible to make simple changes to your desk, car, break room, work schedule, and office supplies. So, rather than focus on the caffeinated energy needed to get you through your rough day, let's look at simple, affordable daily changes to make your work day a little greener and environmentally cleaner.

55. Drive Green and Clean

Before we get into recycling options at work or the best possible energy-efficient tips for your own office or building, we need to focus on the easiest and biggest way to make an everyday difference in your workday: getting there. According to the U.S. Department of Transportation, in 2006 there were 250,851,833 registered vehicles on the highway. Since we already know that more wheels on the road create more pollution, and we all realize that we can't just refuse to go to work, how can we get from point A (home) to point B (work) efficiently, greenly, and simply? The truth is that there just isn't a widely available, convenient, and perfectly green way for every commuter. Yet. You could always go the greenest route and ride your bike, but if you have an hour-long commute, staring down the handlebars at that kind of mileage would be exhausting. However, we are at a very exciting time both politically and environmentally, and with gas prices rising every day, we are all ready for a greener and cheaper option for getting to work. Until that perfect option comes along, of course, there are simple, effective ways to make your trip to work greener, cheaper, and cleaner.

We have already discussed properly maintaining your car, but even if you pamper it with affection, poor driving habits can hinder gas mileage and your green efforts. Here are some gas-saving tips for your morning commute:

- *Set the cruise.* Using cruise control can actually improve your gas mileage by maintaining a steady speed. However, before you get set to cruise, make sure that you are driving on relatively flat land. Hilly terrain can cause the car to accelerate faster than your foot would.

- *Don't have idle thoughts.* Allowing your car to idle for even a short period of time will not only waste gas, but it can also increase pollution. If you are running a quick errand on the way to work, try turning off the car and restarting if you are waiting; consider turning it off and running inside rather than idly waiting at a drive-thru window. Consolidating your errands and working them into your daily commute is a simple way to avoid driving more; however, if you leave your car running while you take care of errands, you are scrapping any positive effects of minimizing your time in the car, and sending your efforts and your pollution straight into the air.

- *Avoid the "Stop and Go."* Avoid stopping and going as much as possible. Sure, this is nearly impossible if you are stuck in rush hour traffic, but there are ways to avoid that. Consider leaving for the office a few minutes earlier to avoid traffic congestion. Use the extra time at work to relax a bit before your daily grind begins. And vice versa for leaving work. Stay behind a few minutes (or leave early if you have that luxury). You can also try mapping out your morning commute by checking out any construction or accident reports. Try calling the Department of Transportation Federal Highway Administration information number (511) to find out about any traffic delays. You can also visit the website www.ops.fhwa.dot.gov/511 for up-to-date information. If your local area isn't available, you can go online and check out your local news, or listen to the Interstate radio station for any possible delays. Taking the time to make your commute more efficient will not only decrease your frustration with sitting in traffic, but also your idling time.

- *Scrape it.* Rather than allowing your car to idle in order to "warm it" on cold days, use a little elbow grease and attempt to scrape the windshield first. The more effort you put into helping your car before making it work, the more your car will help you on your way to work.

- *Lighten your load.* Unload any and all excess weight in your car. The heavier the load in the car, the harder it works to get you places. Make sure to remove any carriers when not in use and avoid carrying around any excess "just in case you need them" items.

- *Air freshen 'er.* On days when air conditioning just isn't so necessary, consider rolling down the windows instead. Enjoy the fresh air and avoid using excess gas and excess energy. However, if you are driving at high speeds on highways, open windows can create excess wind resistance causing your car to actually work harder. So, make smart decisions and roll down the windows when it is best for you and your car. If that isn't an option, consider using the vent to pull in fresh air from outside rather than making your car work harder to cool you.

- *Divide and conquer.* If you are a dual-car family, divvy up those vehicles based on each person's needs. If your drive is longer, then consider taking the more fuel-efficient vehicle and vice versa.

- *Keep it cool.* Buy your gas during the coolest part of the day. Doing so will ensure top fuel quality because your fuel will be at its densest state.

These are only a few simple tips on a very long list of ways to get the most out of your gas and car efficiency. However, once you have mastered these simple techniques, if you are looking for other alternatives, and you are tired of paying through the nose at the pump, then consider these options:

- *Pedal.* If you can, and if you are willing, consider riding a bike to work. Doing so will give your body some exercise, you can avoid all traffic jams, and you will be giving your car a much-needed break.
- *Go Mass-ive.* When possible, and when available, take mass transit to work. A single person who normally has a 20-mile round trip commute can reduce annual CO_2 emissions by 4,800 pounds per year by choosing mass transit over driving to work.
- *Take a dip in the pool.* The carpool, that is! Carpooling reduces congestion and reduces everyday wear and tear on your car. If you can't find someone at work willing to carpool, then consider trying businesses near your work. There is always someone ready and willing to save more money and to improve efficiency. You may also receive added work benefits. (Not to mention the fact that you get to use the cool carpooling lane on the interstate!) Take the time to find out about any potential work benefits you could receive through carpooling. There are no set guidelines or mandatory incentives an employer must offer. However, some of the incentives could be closer parking for those who carpool, reduced charges for parking permits, or early release from work to account for

the added time of taking people home. If your boss isn't on-board, explain that it would reduce the company's parking needs, increase morale, provide more cohesion in the work place, and possibly result in a tax break! That should get the boss's green blood pumping.

• *Go alternative.* Here is where things get really interesting. If you are ready to make a large green change, you can check out the new eco-friendly car options available. However, before you junk your already dependable, reliable, and nearly new car, there are a few things to consider.

Hybrids

With gas prices going through the roof, we are all ready for a change, and exciting, innovative hybrids are considerably more eco-friendly than traditional gas-guzzling cars. But how available, dependable, and affordable are they for every car owner? Now, we aren't knocking hybrids. Far from it. Hybrids are an exciting alternative for going green behind the wheel, and they offer a considerable break at the pump. But, if you are a middle-class, hardworking citizen who needs to conserve your money just as much as you do the Earth's natural resources, hybrids may not be the end-all, be-all answer. First, some hybrids can be more expensive than their nonhybrid cousins. Next, you still have to pay the price at the pump. Not nearly as often, but gas will remain an issue for you. Also, although hybrids are being mass produced and are now in such high demand that they're already being back-ordered, you may still find a lack of knowledgeable mechanics who can work on your car, and you may not know enough about the technology to tinker around with it yourself.

Unlike with a traditional car, when your hybrid battery dies, you shouldn't just pull out the jumper cables to get it going again; you can electrocute yourself or destroy your car in the process. Should your hybrid battery die, you could potentially either need to replace the car, or you may have to shell out $4,000–$5,000 (or more), depending on what kind of hybrid you own, for a new battery. It is also worth noting that since hybrids are so new, the possibility of finding used parts could be daunting. If the original battery begins to fail, would you really want to buy a junked hybrid battery with no guaranteed life left in it? Better yet, would you be able to install it without the help of a highly trained hybrid mechanic? In the past year, eBay has seen an 850 percent increase in sales of used Toyota Prius hybrid batteries. These used batteries are still selling for $450–$1,700. And once you have that $1,700 battery, a dealership mechanic can charge as much as $900 to install it. And batteries may not be your only worry. Even if you experience minor engine troubles, you still need a qualified technician to work on it.

Finally, what happens when that hybrid life expectancy is up? Since they are so new, we have no idea at this point when you can expect your battery to die. Most hybrids have a battery pack warranty of 8–10 years or 100,000–150,000 miles, but with so many used batteries already available, this expectancy cannot be ironclad. It could last longer, but the point is we just don't know. Should your battery die just after that warranty expires, you could be left making payments on a dead battery and/or having to spend money for a new battery. Once that battery dies, how marketable will your "junked" hybrid be? Can you resell it to recoup some of your lost loan money? With such unpredictability, where does that leave you financially?

Hybrids are extremely exciting, the wave of the future, and very tempting. However, before you take out a new loan to get one, check out local repair options as well as availability before you make a large financial decision. With no solid green commuting answers coming to us in the near future concerning oil dependency, adequate amounts of fossil fuels, or even the price of gas, before making a drastic decision that could leave you paying a hefty loan payment, consider making smarter, greener, sensible driving decisions that offer immediate relief without interest rates or delinquency notices.

Ethanol Flex-Fuel Vehicles

Ethanol flexible fuel vehicles (FFVs) are another exciting and growing alternative to traditional gas-powered cars. Although flex-fuel vehicles have been around for a while and are very similar to traditional cars, they are built to run on regular gas or a mixture of 15 percent gasoline and 85 percent ethanol, which is produced from corn, and often classified as biofuel. Although this is a very effective and exciting technology, and it may very well be the contender for hybrids, there are also some things to consider before making the switch to a flex-fuel vehicle.

First, how available is ethanol fuel in your area? Although 10 percent ethanol is currently being pumped into most traditional gas-powered cars, finding a gas station that provides E85—85 percent—the optimal fuel mixture to power a flex-fuel vehicle—could prove more difficult. Also, although biofuels are creating more rural jobs and they are helping reduce our need for foreign oil, more land has to be cleared to create more fuel. Once again, the reaction to an action. While this is also exciting technology, and it is one that needs to be investigated, it remains an alternative rather than a permanent solution.

Hydrogen

Here is a truly exciting option that, according to the Hydrogen Cars website, offers zero-emission technology and is a by-product of water vapor. While the good news is that the government is providing funding, and according to the Hydrogen Cars website, California governor Arnold Schwarzenegger is hoping to have 200 hydrogen stations built by 2010 from Vancouver, British Columbia to Baja, California, the bad news is that these cars are only being experimentally leased at this time, and they are not currently available to every American. Hopefully they may become available in the next few years, but their cost is an unknown factor. The other drawbacks are that hydrogen fuel is produced in a variety of ways: Some include processing algae, others use coal, and still others use methane. If hydrogen is the future, then it is still in the developmental stages, and it still requires processing to create that water vapor reaction.

Although there are fantastic alternatives coming about, at this point in time, they are all still just *alternatives*. For each alterative, there are plusses and minuses. However, with technological teams working in overdrive to meet the demands of the gas-price-gouged citizens, we can be sure that at least one of these options will emerge as the best and greenest possible choice. And who knows? Our technological innovators may eventually come up with a flex-fuel/hydrogen–hybrid. Now that would be worth the back-order wait!

Until that happens, try to make smarter, greener choices to work with what you already have. Remember, you don't have to buy more to make a positive impact on the Earth. Go simple. Reduce your car use when going to work. Share your family car. Carpool. Ride your bike. There are simple, green choices that are already out there and readily available. Rather than go deeper in debt on the potential of technology, why not go green and simple based on everyday conservation choices already at your disposal?

56. Printer Whoas

With deadlines, memos, crunch-time headaches, and projected future goals to plague you at work, the last thing you should be worried about is how you are affecting the environment, right? Since many of us work in one room or office, it would seem that green options would be more for home, school, or even play. Although that is true in some instances, take the time to sit back and think of just how much paper you go through every day. Let's take a look.

Every year, Americans throw away enough office paper to build a 12-foot wall from Los Angeles to New York City. Each person uses approximately one 100-foot-tall Douglas fir tree in paper and wood products every year. And commercial or residential paper waste makes up over 40 percent of waste in landfills. You may be thinking that you use only a few sheets of paper a day, or you may be thinking that, in your job, you are not wasteful. But, how many times do you thoughtlessly print something out? How many memos do you receive/create at work? How many sticky notes do you use? How many receipts do you print/receive? All of us use paper in some form every day, and all of us could reduce that amount in small, easy ways. Here are some suggestions:

- *Print less.* This is obvious, but we have become so used to printing, we often don't realize that we could just store the information in our computer's memory instead. So, before you click on that print icon, stop and decide if it is really necessary. Give your printer, as well as your expensive ink cartridge, a much-needed break.
- *Use both sides.* When you do print, make it double-sided. Making sure that you use every space of the beautiful white, cream, or office gray will ensure that no page is left unturned.

- *Scrap it.* We all need to jot down a little information now and then, so make sure to grab a sheet of scrap paper rather than a crisp new one. This may look and feel messy, but think of it as saving the world, one scribbled note at a time.
- *Reuse envelopes.* When you need to send something, consider using white tape or marking out previous addresses to reuse envelopes. This may feel cheap, but the post office won't mind, and neither will the recipient. After all, they are more interested in what is inside.
- *Increase the e-mail.* Some believe e-mail isn't as formal, but if you take the time to craft it, spell-check it, and edit it, you may make a believer out of the harshest e-mail critics. If your professional e-mail doesn't convince them, tell them you are doing your part to save the trees. That should work. But if you do need to send a hardcopy memo, try to use both sides. And if you receive a hardcopy memo, try to reuse it either for scrap paper or for printing.
- *Use recycled paper.* If you have the freedom to choose which paper you use in your office, consider putting recycled paper on the company's tab. If you have no say in this decision, consider taking up the issue with management. Sure, you may get turned down, but you will feel good about speaking up for an alternative choice. Who knows? You may win the battle, and you may be the very reason that a tree somewhere is breathing a sigh of relief and praising your name in jubilation.
- *Recycle!* We cannot express this enough. It is as simple as putting a bin in your work area and collecting paper to be turned in for recycling. You can ask for permission to start a recycling program at work, or you could just make the personal decision to do it at your desk. Bring a box to work, and col-

lect recyclable trash throughout the day: lunch cartons, sticky notes, newspapers, magazines, or scrap paper. Recycling just 1 ton of paper can save 17 mature trees, 3 cubic yards of space in a landfill, 7,000 gallons of water, 2 barrels of oil, and 4,100 kilowatt-hours of electricity (according to the EPA website). That amount of electricity is enough to power an average home in America for five months.

- *Tissue issues.* Having a cold is always painful whether suffering at home on the couch or braving through a full day at work. Consider using recycled tissues. If you want those extra green points, use a handkerchief. You can always carry more than one if necessary and wash them with your towels and cloth napkins. You will not only save trees, but you may also start a retro trend at work.

That is just a sampling of the ways you can make a difference by being more economical with your paper use. If that doesn't convince you, then consider that, according to the Michigan Department of Environmental Quality, recycling 1 ton of paper typically saves somewhere near $25 to $30 in landfill disposal costs. Not to mention that recycling your paper at work will greatly reduce the air and water pollution from paper manufacturing. Sure, you may not care about the company's expense, but doing your share to reduce expenses may just provide extra company money for your raise.

With papers filling your inbox, unread memos taunting you from your desk, and paperwork mounting in your briefcase, it can be a bit overwhelming to think of cutting back on your use of paper. However, making a few simple and green changes is the first step toward creating big environmental change. Once you make a small change in your use of paper, you will find that what you thought you couldn't live without may just become what you never really miss.

Great Green Tip

To go out for lunch or not to go out for lunch: that is the green workday question. We all enjoy going out to eat, even if it is only for a quick lunch hour. However, consider how much energy you are using to drive somewhere to eat. If you do choose to walk to a nearby restaurant, you are making greener tracks, but always consider the amount of food wasted during your meal. Portions are enormous, and most of us either leave some behind or bring a takeout box back to the office, put it in the break room refrigerator, and then forget it exists. Avoid it all and take your own lunch to work instead. Pack it in a reusable container, take real utensils, and make sure to eat every morsel you take with you. Of course, you don't have to completely give up going out to eat during your workday. What fun is that? But, if you are just grabbing a quick bite, why not make it a green bite? When possible, use your lunch hour to make a greener choice: dine in and catch up with fellow greener colleagues. Maybe you could plan a company meeting about adding recycling bins!

57. A Green Menagerie

Although you are now recycling workers, there are still a few practical and simple tips to apply to your workday in order to make that daily grind a little greener. While using both sides of the paper may seem enough to make a significant dent in the environmental chain, let's not forget the overlooked, and often forgotten, small ways to make a big difference:

- *Turn off your lights.* According to the Sierra Club, 44 percent of the electricity use in offices can be attributed to artificial lighting. You have already gotten into the habit of doing this at home, so bring that good habit to the office as well: Turn off your overhead light when you leave for lunch or at the end of the day. If you have smaller desk lamps, consider replacing your regular bulbs with energy-saving bulbs.

- *Turn off your computer.* Allow your computer to go to "sleep" when you aren't using it. Screensavers will do nothing to save energy. If your company has no policy prohibiting it, consider allowing your computer to hibernate to save more energy.

- *Adjust your thermostat.* If you have the luxury of controlling your own heating or cooling, take the initiative to turn the temperature up in the summer and down in the winter, just as you would at home.

- *Bring a plant.* Just as you need clean, healthy air for your body at home, you need it at work as well. You need your body to function as cleanly and healthily as possible, so green your office with a little hardworking, air-cleaning greenery.

Although these tips are effortless and simple, there are other options out there for those of you that would like to add a little more green to your workday. Many businesses are now on the green highway, realizing the money that can potentially be saved, and responding to employees' demand for greener policies at work. Many employees have no desire to work for companies that are responsible for continuously polluting. Only 41 office buildings in the

United States are LEED (Leadership in Energy and Environmental Design) certified at the platinum level. What that means is that they are fully functioning green office buildings that maximize their use of resources both during and after construction. Some companies may choose to build near a mass transit line for their workers, or use materials that have been recycled. Although this is absolute progress in the workplace, that still leaves countless work environments that haven't been LEED constructed from the ground up.

The good news is that many employers are now getting onboard and offering benefits to employees who make greener efforts at work. Some of these include carpooling benefits, mass transit offerings and discounts, and the option of telecommuting once a week from home.

If your employer hasn't highly advertised such green innovations at work, take the initiative and ask if this may be a direction the company would consider. Using recycled materials, such as computers and furniture, as well as allowing telecommuting whenever possible are real energy savers. Providing green incentives to workers not only increases efficient productivity, but also provides a real sense of pride in one's work. Not only are you working to make a better company, but also a better world.

PART FIVE
Take It to the Streets

Simple ways to sit back, relax, and smell the clean air while on vacation.

One of the greatest joys in life is getting away for that long-awaited, always-anticipated, fun-filled, relaxing vacation. While many of us fantasize about Caribbean waters, hammock naps, couch lounging, television watching, and complete nothingness followed by days of sleep, how many of us plan or spend time considering how to implement green changes for a vacation?

Sound depressing? You spend all this time working, making conscious green choices for your home and your office space, and now we are asking you to take your hard-earned, relaxing, all-inclusive vacation and push it to the wayside for a greener, more simplistic approach to a vacation? Of course not! However, you can still have a fun-filled vacation while making very simple green changes.

So, sit back and read on about how to green your vacation with sly, innovative, and completely effortless green changes. Just make sure to relax and enjoy reading while you plan for your green vacation. You deserve a break, you have been working very hard.

58. Rough It

Okay, admit it, you knew we were going here, right? Before we go any further, we do acknowledge that not every person is an outdoor person. But, what we suggest and advocate is that you give it a try before you resolutely decide that camping will never be your cup of fresh-mountain-water-made tea.

Although you can go back to the basics and backpack into the heart of the wilderness, armed only with your wits, a trusty flashlight, first-aid kit (which we highly recommend on any vacation), and your two-person tent, roughing it to those extremes definitely is not for everyone. There are safer, more comfortable camping amenities available, with showers and nearby restaurants.

To get started, visit www.recreation.gov to find local campgrounds in your area, or www.nps.gov to check out the national park service website. These websites will give you local information about campgrounds as well as break down amenities available at each one. Check out local campgrounds to find places where you and your family can head out, pitch a tent, rent a cabin, or rent a pop-up camper for your outdoor needs. Nearly all campgrounds are affordable, offer fun activities for kids and adults, and often encourage bike riding as the transportation of choice.

If the thought of sleeping in the presence of animals or winged creatures makes your skin crawl, you can always choose to visit a lodge or a resort. However, once you take the time and opportunity to commune with nature, you may find that the beeping, buzzing, and blinking world you left at home won't seem so important as you huddle around the fire that you built with your own two hands (and maybe a few starter logs), roast marshmallows, tell campfire stories, read, relax, and sleep to the sound of peaceful crickets in the distance.

Sure, camping isn't for everyone. But, before you pass on spending time with nature, take a chance and give it a shot. For each camping junkie out there, there are just as many campfire stories starting with, "You know, I used to hate camping until . . ." Go ahead and give it a chance. Once you get out there, smell the fresh air and see the night sky, you may find that you are a little more in tune with nature than you originally thought.

59. Green Service Made to Order

Whether you are a weary traveler, a family vacation gatherer, or a midway, I-need-a-rest grabber, staying in a hotel or a motel can prove efficient, relaxing, and in most instances completely convenient.

However, just how green are hotel visits? There are several simple and green tips you can apply to your hotel stay:

- *Reuse your towels.* It is lovely to have the cleaning service come in to replace those wet towels with plush fresh ones, but just how necessary is it? In order to save energy, try using your

Great Green Tip

Feeling guilty about all the trash you accumulate during your vacations? Fast food containers, hotel cups, napkins and plates, disposable utensils, and take-out dishes. Instead of buying and tossing, consider taking your own cooler full of snacks and mealtime essentials. And, along with your cooler, make sure to pack travel mugs, reusable water bottles, reusable plates, and utensils. You can always wash them when you get to your destination, and you will have the luxury of enjoying your meals outside, possibly picnicking, in the fresh air rather than in a busy, noisy, fast-food restaurant.

towels more than once before allowing the cleaning service to replace them.

- *Skip the cleaning service.* Yes, a made bed is a friendly bed and clean sheets are refreshing, but asking the cleaning staff to skip a day really won't be the end of the world. You will save the staff a little elbow grease, save in cleaning supplies, water use, and the amount of energy and electricity used to wash and dry your dirty linens.

- *Use your own plates.* Continental breakfasts could be the greatest amenity offered by hotels since televisions. It is lovely to simply roll out of bed and have breakfast prepared for you. However, have you ever noticed those pesky foam plates, cups, and bowls, and disposable, well, pretty much everything? Use your own dishes. You already have them packed to use with your cooler, right? Take them with you, grab a cup of brew in your own mug, and eat from your own plates. You will save energy, resources, and landfill space. Just make sure to take your dishes with you when breakfast is over. The hotel staff is accommodating, but not *that* accommodating!

- *Walk to restaurants or shopping areas.* If at all possible, try to find a hotel that is within walking distance of your favorite attractions. Or, see if mass transit is available for you. The less you have to drive, the better for your legs as well as the air quality.
- *Shower in pairs.* That's right! You do it at home, so why not on vacation? Enjoy your time together, even in the shower, all the while saving water and energy.
- *Control your climate.* Just as you do at home, consider saving energy which may allow hotels to drop room rates by turning off the air conditioner when you leave the room. Same goes for heating. If you aren't in there, why heat or cool the room?
- *Recycle.* Yes, even on vacation we urge you to recycle. If your hotel doesn't participate, ask them to direct you to the closest recycling center or bin. Then, fill out a comment card asking your hotel to rethink their recycling choices or lack thereof. And on the flip side, if they do offer recycling as part of your stay, tell them how much you appreciate it.
- *Stay green.* Although not every hotel offers a completely green stay, many are onboard with improving their green amenities. If you would like to patronize only a green hotel, or if you are just interested in seeing price comparisons, try visiting www.allstays.com/green-hotels to gather more information about your green stay.

No matter if you are staying at a five-star hotel or at a lower-priced accommodation, there are many ways to enjoy yourself while still making sure to have that great green attitude and impact wherever you may be. Remember, just because you are taking a break from the world doesn't mean that the world wants you to break away from it.

60. Train Yourself and Your Family

When summertime rolls around and your kids are out of school and you have vacation time begging to be used, and the sand, sun, and crickets are calling, your body can't help but give in to the pull. We all want a chance to get away. And we all, for the most part, deserve it. With gas prices going through the roof, food becoming increasingly more expensive, and the economy being stretched to the breaking point, you may begin to wonder if you can even afford a break. Here we have the obvious question: what is the best way to travel while on vacation?

Of course, your needs depend on your location and your family and time demands, but here are a few simple ways to bring that price of traveling down just enough to possibly enjoy your time away from work:

Keep It Close

How many times have you been shocked to learn that something fun, educational, relaxing, or even just interesting has been only a few miles away from your home all this time? Sometimes we tend to think that the only way to escape life and work is to put thousands of miles between us. Although that is tempting, you can still get away from it all just down the road. Take the time to check out your local attractions before heading to the other side of the country. Just make sure to turn off your cell phone to make yourself less available!

Keep It on the Ground

Although that does seem taxing, and at times frustrating when you can get there twice as fast by flying, planes are still the worst polluters in the transportation chain. If you feel like having an adventure, consider taking a bus tour with a few friends or your entire family. These kinds of trips are still around, and the buses make stops at interesting places while allowing you to relax while someone else takes the wheel.

Keep It Classic

Remember those great movies with passenger trains and dining cars? Those trains still exist! Why not throw your family back in time and take the train rather than drive or fly? The tickets can be expensive, but they often include meals as well as a place to sleep while you hit the rails across the country.

Gone are the days when trains required coal burning furnaces. According to the Amtrak website, the U.S. Department of Energy found that based on energy consumed per passenger mile, Amtrak is 18 percent more energy efficient than flying commercial airlines. That is a pretty significant difference. Also, Amtrak is less vulnerable to crude oil price swings. That is good news for those of us that get fed up with trying to outguess the price of a flight.

Sure, trains are still not a perfect travel solution for having a green vacation, but they do offer a sensible, greener alternative. You could always forsake travel altogether, and just decide to have a "staycation" instead—hang out at your home and have your own camping trip in the backyard. But, if a backyard vacation just isn't in the cards for you, then consider vacationing closer to home or taking the train. Not only will it give you more time away from being behind the wheel to enjoy your family, but you will see the countryside from the luxury of your own window seat on the rail.

61. Tell a Friend

We are at the end of our green vacation together, but before you pack up to go home or book your reservation for next year's family vacation, take the time to tell a friend about your green choices.

Some people will be interested. Some people won't care. Some people will ask for more information. But the only way to get the word out is to speak from experience. Tell your neighbor or fellow camper about how you have become interested in doing something to save the planet. Start a discussion about making your own laundry detergent. You will find, most often, people are looking for a way to do more, and they are most likely discouraged by the thought that saving the world is not only impossible, but also requires very expensive makeovers in order to produce real change. And that can be disappointing and overwhelming.

Be that green light in the dark. Starting a conversation not only opens the forum for questions, debates, and discussions about the necessity for green change in the world, but it also often leads to trading tips and learning more. If your fellow green friend appears interested, become the green authority of your own lifestyle and share your story. Knowledge is power. And, if they are interested, loan them this book about simple and inexpensive ways to go green!

Great Green Tips

Are you looking for an affordable vacation that actively involves the family, provides relaxation, and offers an excellent opportunity to learn more about our environment? A vacation involving ecotourism may be the ticket for you. Ecotourism basically means visiting natural areas in hopes of enjoying and preserving nature as well as focusing on conservational efforts. This type of tourism promotes educational opportunities as well as helps travelers understand the environmental footprint they may leave on an area. Go ahead and plan an eco-friendly, educational vacation. And don't worry, your kids will have so much fun, they will never notice they are learning as well.

Sure, you already recycle in your home, and you are greening your life in small, simple ways. But, there are a couple of options you may have overlooked. Do you have an old cell phone you just can't seem to let go of? What about out-of-date prescription glasses? Donate them! Cell phones for Soldiers, which was started by teenagers Robbie and Brittany Bergquist, accepts donated phones and prepaid calling cards for U.S. soldiers. Since the inception, this program has raised $1 million in donations and has distributed more than 400,000 prepaid calling cards to soldiers overseas. You can also donate your old ones to the Lions Club, which hands them out to children, families, and workers in need.

For more information on cell phone donations, visit www. cellphonesforsoldiers.com/about.html, or for information about donating your glasses, visit www.lionsclubs.org/EN/content/vision_eyeglass_recycling.shtml.

CONCLUSION

Maintain Your Green House

Congratulations! You made it through and hopefully you are bursting with green inspiration, imagination, and a burning desire to start your very own green journey. Although the tips you learned from this book are applicable and very simple, they are merely the tip of the iceberg when it comes to making greener and more energy-efficient choices for our environment.

Hopefully you are ready to get started and to change this world one simple step at a time. However, before you start composting, green cleaning, recycling, and camping, let's remember the basics: Start simple. Start small. Start with what suits you and your family's needs. Once you begin making simple, affordable, and very significant changes to your life, you will see that green living begins to reveal itself to you. Once you feel that a change is seamless and for the most part unnoticed, you will find the desire, ability, and energy to search for new ways to make green changes. And, once your energy bill numbers start falling, and your own kinetic energy starts growing, you will have a green smile on your face, and more money waiting for that rainy day.

The one problem that you may encounter with living green, as with all new changes, is that you may start off full of energy, passion, and drive, which may then fade over time. Green living is not a passing fad. Sure, it is trendy right now, and it is very media worthy. And that, in turn, can create pressure to make fast changes, big changes, and short-lived changes. Who hasn't tried that faddish crash diet for a few weeks, only to get frustrated, disappointed, and completely ravished with hunger before chucking it out the window? We all do it.

The best way to ensure that green living becomes second nature in your home is to make it a part of your family life. Let's look at it like this: Imagine your green lifestyle is similar to maintaining a clean house. There are two approaches to cleaning a home. You can attack it with random bursts of energy. ("No one call me for a week. I will be cleaning.") Then fall, exhausted, onto the couch where you lie in cleaning hibernation for months at a time. Your home will be clean, but it isn't easy to muster that strength to do it again, and mounting a fast and furious attack can leave you frustrated and dreading the next round of cleaning. The other approach is to maintain it, little by little, doing small, easy, daily tasks, divided among and focusing on involving the entire family along the way. This keeps it steady, clean, and functioning while still leaving time for play and relaxation.

We believe the easiest way to maintain a clean house, and a green house, is to do a little at a time, do what is best for you, and do it as you go. Not only does cleaning become effortless after a while, but it also becomes a part of your everyday life. With the same approach to making simple, green changes, after doing it for so long, it will become your "lifestyle" rather than your "green lifestyle."

We can't emphasize enough that although many of these tips are easy and very user-friendly, some of them just may not be for you. That is okay. There is no shame and no fault in realizing that you can't do it all. None of us is perfect. And none of us is a perfect environmentalist. You, as your own person, need to make the best green decisions for you and your family. That will ensure that you live a green, productive, and *happy* life rather than a high-maintenance, unaffordable, overly green, faddish lifestyle.

It is important to understand that every new change in life comes with just as many setbacks before you can move forward.

Although it is very important to give yourself praise for making this important decision, it is also necessary to give yourself room to fail. You will attempt to make a green change, want it to happen with all your heart, only to realize that it just doesn't work for you and your family. We wanted to use cloth diapers. We were determined to avoid the use of disposable diapers and were outraged by the number of diapers that end up in our landfills. Until we faced our first raging diaper rash, wailing baby, and soiled floor. Not to mention the amount of water, energy, and detergent needed to clean those environmentally friendly diapers. Yes, we failed. And that is okay. You will fail, too, at times, and it is important to pick yourself up, dust yourself off, and start all over again, knowing that the green changes that you are making and continue to make will create fantastic and significant global change.

Remember, you aren't in this to compete with your newly green neighbor. And you aren't in this for anyone other than yourself and your family, so don't allow the green naysayers out there to convince you to stray from your goals. Yes, they are out there: The people who feel guilty that they aren't doing something, so they want to disparage you for doing what you can. They will attack you when you do not meet their expectations for what they think you should be doing. So, when your intruding neighbor says, "You know, for a person living a green lifestyle, you really shouldn't be driving as much as you do," you can say, with a pleasant smile, "You're right! I'm not doing everything. But, I am doing something." And that is what will ultimately keep our world green and happy.

NOTES

38 Goodyear, Charlie. "S.F. First City to Ban Plastic Shopping Bags." *San Francisco Chronicle*. March 28, 2007.

39 Natural Resource Defence Council website. "NRDC Lauds Passage of New York City Council Legislation Requiring Groceries, Retailers to Provide Plastic Bag Recycling for Consumers." January 9, 2008.

42 Goldberg, Bob. "The Hyprocrisy of Organic Farmers." Posted on AgBioWorld website, which is dedicated to focusing on agricultural biotechnology, June 5, 2000.

53 Reed, Jim, and Denver Water (courtesy of Liz Gardener). "Dishwasher Water Use—Facts and Figures." American Water Works Association website, December 2005.

56 "Municipal Solid Waste Generation, Recycling, and Disposal in the United States: Facts and Figures for 2006," an EPA study.

66 Arnold, Emily, and Larsen, Janet. "Bottled Water: Pouring Resources Down the Drain." Earth Policy Institute website. February 2, 2006.
Driessen, Suzanne [Regional Extension Educator, Food Science]. "Water Bottle Safety." University of Minnesota Extension Food Safety website. October 1, 2003.
Takeuchi, Cullen, Lisa. "Freshen Up Your Drink." *Time*. March 24, 2008.

67 POV borders/environment PBS "Not Disposable Anymore." Public Broadcasting System (PBS) website.

73 Holmes, Gary. "Nielsen Media Research Reports Television's

Popularity Is Still Growing." Nielsen Media Research web-site. September 21, 2006.

92 Chudler, Dr. Eric. "What is sleep . . . and why do we need it?" Neuroscience for Kids website.

96 State of Utah. "Division of Water Resources." Utah State website. 2007.

118 Dunn, Collin. "Make Your Own Laundry Soap." The Planet Green website. March 23, 2008.

119 Findley, Mary. "Safe, Natural Green Cleaning Supplies & Cleaning Products." Mary Moppins website. 2008.

125 Green Car Congress website.
Florida Department of Highway Safety and Motor Vehicles website. "Buying or Selling a Car." 2008.

146 Battery Disposal Guide. Environmental Health and Safety website.

147 EPA. "Implementation of the Mercury-Containing and Rechargable Battery Management Act." EPA brochure. November 1997.

149 EPA. "Municipal Solid Waste Generation Recycling and Disposal in the United States, Facts and Figures." June 4, 2008.
Martin, Andrew. "One Country's Table Scraps, Another Country's Meal." New York Times. May 18, 2008.

156 Howard, Brian Clark. "Back-to-School Green Shopping Guide." The Daily Green website. July 20, 2008.

166 Mello, Tara Baukus. "Top 10 Tips for Improving Your Fuel Economy." Edmund's website. June 4, 2008.

168 "Public Transportation Reduces Greenhouse Gases and Conserves Energy," a study. American Public Transportation Association website. July 19, 2008.

170 Naughton, Keith. "Assaulted Batteries." Newsweek. May 27, 2008.

171 Grunwald, Michael. "The Clean Energy Scam." *Time*.
     April 2008.

173 "Waste Reduction and Recyling Waste Facts and Figures."
     Clean Air Council website. July 19, 2008.
     "Environmental Benefits of Recycle on the Go." EPA web-
     site. April 8, 2008.
     Michigan Department of Environmental Quality website.
     "Reducing Office Paper Waste." May 2004.

177 Takeuchi Cullen, Lisa. "Going Green at the Office." *Time*.
     June 7, 2007.

RESOURCES

Chapter 2: Squash the Litterbug

Keep America Beautiful:
www.kab.org

Green-CT, "Litter facts":
www.greenct.org/litter.htm

Natural Resources Defense Council, "Make Waves":
www.nrdc.org/makewaves/makewaves.pdf (July 1, 2008)

Physorg, "Giant garbage patch floating in Pacific," Oct. 22, 2007:
www.physorg.com/news112248742.html

Algalita Marine Research Foundation, "Plastics Are Forever,"
AMRF brochure on the Web:
algalita.org/pdf/plastics%20are%20forever%20english.pdf
(February 3, 2008)

Chapter 4: Get an Old Set of Wheels

The Union of Concerned Scientists, "Clean Vehicles":
www.ucsusa.org/clean_vehicles/vehicles_health/cars-trucks-air-pollution.html (July 19, 2008)

Chapter 5: Green Grass Pass

EPA, "Outdoor Air-Transportation: Lawn Equipment-Additional Information":
www.epa.gov/air/community/details/yearequip_addl_info.html
(February 12, 2008)

EPA, "Your Yard and Clean Air," EPA information handout on the Web:
www.epa.gov/otaq/consumer/19-yard.pdf (July 19, 2008)

Chapter 6: Green Means Stop

EPA, "Water Efficient Landscaping: Preventing Pollution and Using Resources," EPA brochure on the Web:
www.epa.gov/WaterSense/docs/water-efficient_landscaping_508.pdf
(July 19, 2008)

Chapter 8: Pile It Up

Compost Guide, "A Complete Guide to Composting":
www.compostguide.com (June 1, 2008)

Chapter 9: Plant a Tree

The Food and Agriculture Organization of the United Nations, "Facts and Figures, FAO Resources Assessment 2005":
www.fao.org/forestry/30515/en (April 21, 2008)

Maryland Department of Natural Resources, "Trees Reduce Air Pollution":
www.dnr.state.md.us/forests/publications/urban2.html
(July 19, 2008)

Chapter 14: It's in the Bag

Charlie Goodyear, "S.F. First City to Ban Plastic Shopping Bags: Supermarkets and chain pharmacies will have to use recyclable or compostable sacks," *San Francisco Chronicle* on the Web, March 28, 2007:
www.sfgate.com/cgi-bin/article.cgi?file=/c/a/2007/03/28/MNGDROT5QN1.DTL (July 19, 2008)

Natural Resources Defense Council, "NRDC Lauds Passage of New York City Council Legislation Requiring Groceries, Retailers to Provide Plastic Bag Recycling for Consumers," NRDC Media Center on the Web, Press contact: Jenny Powers, January 9, 2008:
www.nrdc.org/media/2008/080109.asp (June 14, 2008)

Chapter 15: Buy "Ourganically"

Natural Resources Defense Council, "Issues, Health," October 11, 2002:
www.nrdc.org/health/farming/forg101.asp (March 3, 2008)

Bob Goldberg, "The Hypocrisy of Organic Farmers," *Ag Bio World* newsletter on the Web, June 5, 2005:
www.agbioworld.org/biotech-info/articles/biotech-art/hypocrisy.html (March 1, 2008)

Chapter 17: Dine and Dab with Cloth

Natural Resources Defense Council, "Shop Smart Save Forests":
www.nrdc.org/land/forests/tissueguide/walletcard.pdf
(January 22, 2008)

Chapter 18: Doctor Your Fridge and Freezer

Energy Efficiency and Renewable Energy, "Refrigerators," January 21, 2008:
www1.eere.energy.gov/consumer/tips/refrigerators.html

Chapter 19: Ditch Disposable Dishes

Alliance of Foam Packaging Recyclers, "EPS Recycling":
www.epspackaging.org/info.html (July 19, 2008)

Earth 911:
earth911.org/ (July 19, 2008)

EPA, "10 Fast Facts on Recycling," July 19, 2008:
www.epa.gov/reg3wcmd/solidwasterecyclingfacts.htm

Chapter 20: Sit Back and Get Lazy

Jim Reed, Denver Water (courtesy of Liz Gardener), "Dishwasher Water Use—Facts and Figures," Water Wiser on the Web, December 2001:
www.awwa.org/waterwiser/watch/index.cfm?ArticleID=30
(July 19, 2008)

Natural Resource Defense Council's, "Issues: Laundrycare":
www.nrdc.org/enterprise/greeningadvisor/wq-laundry.asp
(July 19, 2008).

Chapter 21: Turn It In

EPA, "Municipal Solid Waste Generation, Recycling, and Disposal in the United States: Facts and Figures for 2006," November 2007:
www.epa.gov/epaoswer/non-hw/muncpl/pubs/msw06.pdf
(July 19, 2008)

Chapter 24: Get Off the Bottle

Union of Concerned Scientists, "Green Tips: Is Bottled Water Better," June 2007:
www.ucsusa.org/publications/greentips/is-bottled-water-better.html

Container Recycling Institute's, "Bottled Water":
www.container-recycling.org/plasfact/bottledwater.htm
(July 19, 2008)

Emily Arnold and Janet Larsen, "Bottled Water: Pouring Resources Down the Drain," Earth Policy Institute website, February 2, 2006:
www.earth-policy.org/Updates/2006/Update51_printable.htm

Suzanne Driessen, "Water Bottle Safety," Regional Extension Educator, Food Science, October 1, 2003:
www.extension.umn.edu/foodsafety/components/columns/Oct2.htm (July 19, 2008)

Lisa Takeuchi Cullen, "Freshen Up Your Drink," *Time* Magazine on the Web, Thursday, March 13, 2008:
www.time.com/time/magazine/article/0,9171,1722266,00.html

EPA, "Consumer Confidence Report," July 6, 2006:
www.epa.gov/safewater/ccr/index.html

PBS, "Not Disposable Anymore":
www.pbs.org/pov/borders/2004/water/water_disposable.html
(November 22, 2007)

Chapter 25: Expose Electronic Ghosts

Department of Energy, "Appliances and Electronics":
www.energy.gov/applianceselectronics.htm (February 3, 2008)

Chapter 26: See the Light

ENERGY STAR, "Lightbulbs and Fixtures":
www.energystar.gov/index.cfm?c=lighting.pr_lighting
(July 19, 2008)

EERE, "DOE Seeks a Fast Track to New Energy Efficiency
Standards," February 28, 2007, EERE Network News on the Web:
www.eere.energy.gov/news/archive.cfm/pubDate=%7Bd%20'2007
-02-28'%7D#10596

Chapter 27: Squeeze the Tube

Gary Holmes, "Nielsen Media Research Reports Television's
Popularity Is Still Growing," Nielsen Media Research on the
Web, September 21, 2006;
www.nielsenmedia.com/nc/portal/site/Public/menuitem.
55dc65b4a7d5adff3f65936147a062a0/?vgnextoid=
4156527aacccd010VgnVCM100000ac0a260aRCRD

Chapter 31: Light Your Green Fire

EERE, "Fireplaces," May 31, 2006:
www1.eere.energy.gov/consumer/tips/fireplaces.html

Great Green Tip

Medical University of South Carolina, "Tips for a Green Holiday Season," Office of Recycling and Solid Waste Management: www.musc.edu/recycle/holidays.htm (July 19, 2008)

Chapter 33: Don't Let the Energy Bugs Bite

EERE, "Space Heating and Cooling," September 12, 2005: www.eere.energy.gov/consumer/your_home/space_heating_cooling/index.cfm/mytopic=12300

EERE, "Thermostats and Control Systems," January 11, 2008: www.eere.energy.gov/consumer/your_home/space_heating_cooling/index.cfm/mytopic=12720

EERE, "Ceiling Fans and Other Circulating Fans," January 11, 2008:
www.eere.energy.gov/consumer/your_home/space_heating_cooling/index.cfm/mytopic=12355

Chapter 35: Take the Time to Smell the Houseplants

Neuroscience for Kids:
faculty.washington.edu/chudler/sleep.html (June 6, 2008)

EPA, "An Introduction to Air Quality," July 19, 2008: www.epa.gov/iaq/ia-intro.html

Clean Air Gardening, "Top Houseplants for Improving Indoor Air Quality":
www.cleanairgardening.com/houseplants.html (July 19, 2008)

Chapter 36: Put On Your Green Shower Cap

California Energy Commission (Consumer Energy Center), "Shower vs Bath":
www.consumerenergycenter.org/myths/shower_vs_bath.html (July 19, 2008)

State of Utah Website, Utah.gov, "Bathroom Water Use":
conservewater.utah.gov/IndoorUse/Bathroom (July 19, 2008)

Chapter 37: Unflush Your Money Down the Drain

EPA, "WaterSense Labeled Toilets," July 17, 2008:
www.epa.gov/WaterSense/pubs/het.htm

EPA, "Indoor Water in the United States," July 19, 2008:
www.epa.gov/WaterSense/pubs/indoor.htm

Chapter 38 The Tooth of It All

EPA, "High-Efficiency Bathroom Sink Faucets," July 17, 2008:
www.epa.gov/watersense/pubs/bathroom_faucets.htm

Chapter 40: Everything but the Bathroom Sink

Eco-Action, "Pollution":
www.eco-action.net/pollution.html (July 19, 2008)

Chapter 42: Tumble Dry Lowdown

Simple Steps, "Clean, Fresh and Energy Efficient," Nov 14, 2007:
www.simplesteps.org/content/view/0/188/37

EERE, "Laundry," January 21, 2008:
www1.eere.energy.gov/consumer/tips/laundry.html

Chapter 43: A Mixed Load of Laundry Tips

Collin Dunn, "Make Your Own Laundry Soap," Planet Green,
March 23, 2008:
planetgreen.discovery.com/home-garden/make-your-own-laundry-
soap.html

Coalition for Clean Air, "Hung Out to Dry, Getting Toxins Out
of Dry Cleaning":
www.coalitionforcleanair.org/news-fact-sheets-Hung-Out-to-Dry-
Cleaning-Up-Dry-Cleaning.html#Perchloroethylene
(July 19, 2008)

EPA, "Frequently Asked Questions about Dry Cleaning,"
December 19, 2007:
www.epa.gov/dfe/pubs/garment/ctsa/factsheet/ctsafaq.htm#1

Mary Findley, "Stain Removal Guide: Baby Clothes," Mary
Moppins on the Web:
www.GoClean.com (July 19, 2008)

Chapter 44: Get Out of Hot Water

EERE, "Water Heating Tips," January 21, 2008:
www1.eere.energy.gov/consumer/tips/water_heating.html

American Council for an Energy Efficient Economy,
"Consumer's Guide to Home Energy Savings: Condensed Online
Version—Water Heating," August 2007:
www.aceee.org/consumerguide/waterheating.htm#minimize

Chapter 45: Behind Closed Garage Doors

EPA, "Tips to Improve Gas Mileage," August 1994:
www.epa.gov/otaq/consumer/17-tips.pdf

Fuel Economy, "Keeping Your Car in Shape":
www.fueleconomy.gov/feg/maintain.shtml (June 29, 2008)

Green Car Congress, "Study: Nearly 35% of Households Have at
Least Three," Green Car Congress on the Web, February 12, 2008:
www.greencarcongress.com/2008/02/study-nearly-35.html

EDF, "Return Trip: How to Recycle the Family Car,"
Environmental Defense Fund on the Web, August 15, 2007:
www.edf.org/article.cfm?contentID=2195

Florida DMV, "Buying or Selling a Car":
hsmv.state.fl.us/dmv/usedcar.html (July 19, 2008)

Fuel Economy, "Keeping Your Car in Shape":
www.fueleconomy.gov/feg/maintain.shtml (July 19, 2008)

Chapter 46: Insulate Your Bank Account

EERE, "Adding Insulation to an Existing Home,"
September 12, 2005:
www.eere.energy.gov/consumer/your_home/insulation_
airsealing/index.cfm/mytopic=11350

ENERGY STAR, "Do It Yourself Guide to Sealing Air Leaks
and Adding Insulation with ENERGY STAR," ENERGY
STAR brochure on the Web, August 2007:
www.energystar.gov/ia/home_improvement/home_sealing/DIY_
COLOR_100_dpi.pdf

Chapter 47: Your Green Foundation

EERE, "Basement Insulation," September 19, 2005:
www.eere.energy.gov/consumer/your_home/insulation_
airsealing/index.cfm/mytopic=11470

ENERGY STAR, "Damp Basement":
www.energystar.gov/index.cfm?c=home_solutions.hm_
improvement_dampbasement (March 3, 2008)

Chapter 50: Toy with It

Environment, Health and Safety, "Battery Recycling and Disposal
Guide for Households," July 19, 2008:
www.ehso.com/ehshome/batteries.php

EPA, "Implementation of the Mercury-Containing and
Rechargeable Battery Management Act," EPA brocure on the
Web, November 1997:
www.epa.gov/epaoswer/hazwaste/recycle/battery.pdf

Chapter 51: Put the F-U-N Back in the Family Functions

EPA, "Municipal Solid Waste Generation, Recycling, and Disposal
in the United States, Facts and Figures for 2006," EPA study
on the Web, November 2007:
www.epa.gov/garbage/pubs/msw06.pdf

Chapter 53: Too Green for School

Brian Clark Howard, "Back-to-School Green Shopping Guide," Daily Green, July 19, 2008:
www.thedailygreen.com/going-green/5264

Patricia Monahan, "School Bus Pollution Report Card 2006," UCUSA publication on the Web, May 2006:
www.ucsusa.org/assets/documents/clean_vehicles/pollution-report-card-2006.pdf

Chapter 55: Drive Green and Clean

Bureau of Transportation Statistics, "Table 1-11: Number of U.S. Aircraft, Vehicles, Vessels, and Other Conveyances":
www.bts.gov/publications/national_transportation_statistics/html/table_01_11.html (July 19, 2008)

Tara Baukus Mello, "Top 10 Tips for Improving Your Fuel Economy," Edmunds.com:
www.edmunds.com/reviews/list/top10/103164/article.html (June 4, 2008)

American Public Transportation Association, "Public Transportation Reduces Greenhouse Gases and Conserves Energy":
www.apta.com/research/info/online/greenhouse_brochure.cfm (July 19, 2008).

We Can Solve the Climate Crisis, "Save money and the climate: carpooling 101":
www.wecansolveit.org/content/pages/16 (July 6, 2008)

Keith Naughton, "Assaulted Batteries, Hybrids Are Hot but Some Drivers Are Concerned about the High Cost of Saving That Gas-saving Battery," *Newsweek* on the Web, May 27, 2008:
www.newsweek.com/id/138808?from=rss

Brock Yates, "Hybrid Issues and a Rising Star at Indy," *Car and Driver* online, September 2005:
www.caranddriver.com/features/columns/c_d_staff/brock_yates/hybrid_issues_and_a_rising_star_at_indy_column

Michael Grunwald, "The Clean Energy Scam," *Time* Magazine Online, March 27, 2008:
www.time.com/time/magazine/article/0,9171,1725975-2,00.html

Hydrogen Cars:
www.hydrogencarsnow.com (July 10, 2008)

Chapter 56: Printer Whoas

Michigan Dept. of Environmental Quality, "Reducing Office Paper Waste," May 2004:
www.deq.state.mi.us/documents/deq-ead-recycle-redofcpw.pdf

Clean Air Council, "Waste Reduction and Recycling Waste Facts and Figures":
www.cleanair.org/Waste/wasteFacts.html (July 19, 2008)

EPA, "Environmental Benefits of Recycle on the Go," April 8, 2008:
www.epa.gov/rcc/onthego/benefits/index.htm#paper

Chapter 57: A Green Menagerie

Sierra Club, "10 Ways to Go Green at Work," The Green Life, March 8, 2007:
sierraclub.typepad.com/greenlife/2007/03/10_ways_to_go_g.html (July 19, 2008)

Lisa Takeuchi Cullen, "Going Green at the Office," *Time* Magazine on the Web, June 7, 2007:
www.time.com/time/magazine/article/0,9171,1630552,00.html

Chapter 60: Train Yourself and Your Family

Amtrak, "Energy Efficient Travel":
www.amtrak.com/servlet/ContentServer?pagename=
Amtrak/am2Copy/Title_Image_Copy_Page&cid=
1093554056875&c=am2Copy&ssid=565 (July 19, 2008)

ADDITIONAL READING

Chapter 2: Squash the Litterbug

Eric Lanford, "Garbage Island," CNN video on the Web, April 14, 2008: www.cnn.com/video/#/video/bestoftv/2008/04/14/ntm.garbage. island.cnn?iref=videosearch

Chapter 3: Plant a Garden

Sharon Lovejoy, *Roots Shoots Buckets and Boots: Gardening Together with Children* (New York: Workman Publishing Company, May 1999). Visit www.gardenweb.com/vl for a virtual web of countless gardening links.

Chapter 7: Weed Out the Pests

Pioneer Thinking, "Garden Pests and Problems": www.pioneerthinking.com/garden-pests.html (July 19, 2008)

Marie Suzanne, "Daylillies 101 part 4," Daily Weeder, July 12, 2007: www.dailyweeder.com/?s=tablespoons&paged=2 (July 19, 2008)

Eric Vinje, "Natural Born Pest Killers," *Planet Natural*: www.planetnatural.com/site/xdpy/kb/natural-pest-controls.html (July 19, 2008)

Barbara Ellis and Fern Marshall Bradley (eds.), *The Organic Gardener's Handbook of Natural Insect and Disease Control: A Complete Problem-Solving Guide to Keeping Your Garden and Yard Healthy Without Chemicals*, (Rodale Books, May 15, 1996).

Sharon Lovejoy, *Trowel & Error: Over 700 Shortcuts, Tips & Remedies for the Gardener*, (New York: Workman Publishing, February 2003).

Chapter 8: Pile It Up

EPA, "Create Your Own Compost Pile," July 19, 2008: www.epa.gov/composting/by_compost.htm (July 20, 2008)

Chapter 9: Plant a Tree

Arbor Day Foundation: www.arborday.org (January 21, 2008)

Chapter 11: Recycle Your Memories

Greg Der Ananian, *Bazaar Bizarre: Not Your Granny's Crafts!* (New York: Viking Studio, a member of The Penguin Group, 2005).

Jessica Vitkus, *AlternaCrafts: 20+: Hi-Style Lo-Budget Projects to Make* (New York: Stewart Tabori and Chang).

Geocities.com, "Darling Creations": www.geocities.com/Heartland/Grove/3870/index.html (January 21, 2008)

Garden Web, "Garden Junk," a Web community for gardening ideas: forums2.gardenweb.com/forums/junk (January 21, 2008)

Chapter 15: Buy "Ourganically"

National Pesticide Information Center, "Information Fact Sheet": npic.orst.edu/npicfact.htm (July 19, 2008)

USDA, "Residue Violator List," July 1, 2008:
www.fsis.usda.gov/PDF/Residue_Violators_List.pdf
(January 21, 2008)

Chapter 18: Doctor Your Fridge and Freezer

USDA, "Refrigeration and Food Safety," November 2005:
www.fsis.usda.gov/Fact_Sheets/Refrigeration_&_Food_Safety/
index.asp#13

Chapter 21: Turn It In

Recycling Centers.org:
www.recyclingcenters.org (November 3, 2008)

Chapter 24: Get Off the Bottle

NRDC, "Consumer Guide to Water Filters, How to find the right water filter for your home," August 16, 2005:
www.nrdc.org/water/drinking/gfilters.asp

Chapter 26: See the Light

EERE, "Estimating Appliance and Home Electronic Energy Usage," September 12, 2005:
www.eere.energy.gov/consumer/your_home/appliances/
index.cfm/mytopic=10040

Chapter 38: The Tooth of It All

Sbwater.org, "House Tips for Saving Water":
www.sbwater.org/HomeConservation.htm (July 20, 2008)

Chapter 39: Go Natural and Green Clean

Annie B. Bond, "How To Make a Non-Toxic Cleaning Kit,"
Care2 on the Web, September 30, 1999:
www.care2.com/greenliving/make-your-own-non-toxic-
cleaning-kit.html

Annie Berthold-Bond, *Clean and Green: The Complete Guide to Non-Toxic and Environmentally Safe Housekeeping* (Woodstock, New York: Ceres Press, 1994).

Geocities.com, "Clean and Green":
www.geocities.com/Heartland/Prairie/8088/clngrn.html

Noel Marie Taylor, "27 Ways to Clean with Baking Soda," *The New Homemaker*:
www.thenewhomemaker.com/bakingsoda (July 19, 2008)

P.W. McRandle, "DIY Household Cleaners," Green Guide on the Web, #120, May/June 2007:
www.thegreenguide.com/doc/120/diy

Chapter 40: Everything but the Bathroom Sink

USDA, "National Organic Program," July 15, 2008:
www.ams.usda.gov/nop/NOP/standards/LabelPre.html

Chapter 45: Behind Closed Garage Doors

Fuel Economy.gov, "Find a Car:"
www.fueleconomy.gov/feg/find acar.htm (July 19, 2008)

Green California,"Vehicles/Transportation: Retreaded Tires":
www.green.ca.gov/EPP/vehicles/RetreadedTires.htm#resources
(July 19, 2008)

Chapter 46: Insulate Your Bank Account

Department of Energy, "Zip Code Insulation Program":
www.ornl.gov/~roofs/Zip/ZipHome.html (July 19, 2008)

Chapter 47: Your Green Foundation

EERE, "Basement Insulation," September 19, 2005:
www.eere.energy.gov/consumer/your_home/insulation_
airsealing/index.cfm/mytopic=11470

Department of Energy, "R-Value Recommendations":
www.ornl.gov/sci/roofs%2bwalls/insulation/ins_16.html
(July 19, 2008)

ENERGY STAR, "Air Seal and Insulate with ENERGY STAR":
www.energystar.gov/index.cfm?c=home_sealing.hm_improvement
_sealing (July 19, 2008)

Chapter 51: Put the F-U-N Back in the Family Functions

Andrew Martin, "One Country's Table Scraps, Another Country's
Meal," *New York Times* on the Web, May 18, 2008:
www.nytimes.com/2008/05/18/weekinreview/18martin.html?_r=
1&oref=slogin&pagewanted=all

Chapter 53: Too Green for School

Sarah Young, "More exhaust inhaled by kids inside school buses than by others in the area, says study," University of California, UC Newsroom on the Web, April 4, 2005:
www.universityofcalifornia.edu/news/article/7037

Iowa State University, "Hybrid School Buses Hit the Road; Researchers Test Their Performance," *ScienceDaily*, January 20, 2008:
www.sciencedaily.com/releases/2008/01/080116164246.htm

The Green Schools Initiative, "This Little Green School House," The Green Schools Initiative publication on the Web:
www.greenschools.net/execsummary.pdf (July 19, 2008)

Chapter 54: Let Them Take the Reins

Keep America Beautiful:
www.kab.org/site/PageServer?pagename=index (July 19, 2008)

Habitat for Humanity:
www.habitat.org (July 19, 2008)

Chapter 55: Drive Green and Clean

Fuel Economy.gov, "Driving More Efficiently":
www.fueleconomy.gov/feg/driveHabits.shtml (July 19, 2008)

EPA, "Your Car and Clean Air: What You Can Do to Reduce Pollution," Office of Mobile Sources brochure on the Web, August 1994:
www.epa.gov/otaq/consumer/18-youdo.pdf

AAA, "Fuel Saving Tips":
www.aaa.com/aaa/215/automotive/fuel/tips.htm (July 19, 2008)

Chapter 56: Printer Whoas

Sierra Club, "10 Ways to Go Green at Work," *The Green Life*, March 8, 2007:
sierraclub.typepad.com/greenlife/2007/03/10_ways_to_go_g.html

Resource Conservation Alliance, "Using Less Wood," Resource Conservation Alliance information handout on the Web:
www.woodconsumption.org/products/paper.pdf (July 19, 2008)

Kim McKay, Tim Wallace, and Jenny Bonnin, *True Green@Work: 100 Ways You Can Make the Environment Your Business* (National Geographic Society, February 1, 2008).

Chapter 60: Train Yourself and Your Family

Amtrak:
www.amtrak.com (July 19, 2008)

AAA, "Fuel Cost Calculator":
www.fuelcostcalculator.com (July 19, 2008)

Great Green Tip—Vacationing

Recreation.gov:
www.recreation.gov (July 19, 2008)

National Park Service:
www.nps.gov (July 19, 2008)

Nature Conservancy, "What Is Eco-tourism":
www.nature.org/aboutus/travel/ecotourism/about/art667.
html   (July 19, 2008)

INDEX

Accommodations, hotels, 181–83
Aerators, 101–2
AgBioWorld, 42
Agribusiness, 41–44
Air conditioners, 87, 166
Air conditioning. *See* Heating and cooling
Air filters, auto, 124
Air filtration system, 93
Air fresheners, 166
Air pollution, 13–15, 92, 164
Alarm clocks, 89
Algalita Marine Research Foundation (AMRF), 10, 195
Alternative wrapping paper, 83–84
American Forests, 143
American Water Works Association, 53
Amtrak, 186
Aphids, 20
Apple cider vinegar, for debugging, 62
Arbor Day Foundation, 143
Arts and craft projects, 136–43
    Dry-Erase Doodle Pages, 141–42
    Fridge Poetry, 138
    Green Flash Cards, 140–41
    Green Paper Dolls, 139–40
    Green Placemats, 137
    Green Shopping List, 142–43
    magazine stool, 80–81
    matchless socks, 115
    planting centerpiece, 29–30

    Recycled Greeting Cards, 138–39
    soda bottle terrarium, 60–61
    stained-glass project, 63–65
    stepping stones, 30–31
    window boxes, 19
Attic insulation, 127–28
Automobiles, 123–26, 165–72
    biking versus driving, 13–14, 124
    buying tips, 125–26
    ethanol flexible fuel vehicles, 171
    gas-saving tips, 165–68
    hybrid, 169–71
    hydrogen-fuel, 171–72
    maintenance of, 124
    recycling, 125

Baby formula stains, 119
Baby gifts, 151
Baby-sitting coupons, 151
Backpacking, 180–81
Backyard green tips, 5–32
    bicycling, 13–14
    branching out, 7–9
    bringing the outdoors inside, 75–76
    composting, 22–25
    lawn care, 14–19
    planting a garden, 11–13
    recycling rainwater, 28
    recycling your memories (craft projects), 29–31
    squashing the litterbug, 9–11